This Is Why You're Single

Aaron Lamont Curry

AL,
YOU'VE ALWAYS BEEN LIKE A FATHER FIGURE
TO ME! IT WAS SO NICE TO SEE YOU AND
RECONNECT, MUCH LOVE AND MANY BLESSINGS
TO YOU AND YOUR FAMILY!

—

Seraph Books

www.seraphbooks.com

This Is Why You're Single

THIS IS WHY YOU'RE SINGLE
-Copyright © 2014, Aaron Lamont Curry

Cover Design By: Alyssa M. Curry
Copy Editor: Alyssa M. Curry
Cover Photo By: Fred Fokkelman
Author Photo: Gerry Garcia

ISBN Paperback: 978-1-941711-05-7
ISBN E-Book: 978-1-941711-06-4
Library of Congress: 2014951813

For information regarding special discounts for bulk purchases of this book for educational, gift purposes, as a charitable donation, or to arrange a speaking event, please visit: www.seraphbooks.com

www.aaronlamont.com
twitter@iammrac
www.facebook.com/aaron.lamont.7

Dedication

Thank you God for the abundance of blessings and gift of life you have given me. Thank you for all you've allowed me to see, experience and learn.

To the women who taught me how to treat women the way they deserve to be treated, my mom and baby sister, Alyssa Curry.

Acknowledgements

Thank you to all of the women that participated in my studies, polls and situational questions in order for me to solicit specific data and analysis for *This Is Why You're Single*. My goal is for this information to help facilitate better understanding between men and women. Utilizing a melting pot of ethnicities, the topic of being single is meant to cross invisible boundaries of race and cultures.

Thank you to the countless men that offered personal situations and insightful information to help bring understanding as to why women are single and what needs to change to bring us together for the right reasons.

Thank you to those that participated and allowed me the permission to share the stories in this book.

Thank you to the women that allowed me to be a part of their life. Whether it was friendship or intimacy that was shared, my experiences with you are what helped shape my ideas surrounding love, relationships and life experiences in general.

Matt, I love you like a brother. You have always been there for me and I know that will never change, as your loyalty is transcendental. Thank you for being the older brother I never had. You are truly a part of my family.

Baby sister; thank you for your work on this project. You have the most amazing spirit and unwearied soul of anyone I've known. Your love and compassion for life and others is infinite, just as my love for you. Never change, for anyone.

Jeff, I love you. You've been in my life for just a few years and have made an unexplainable impact on me. Thank you for all of your fatherly advice.

Lastly, I would like to thank my mother for raising me to be the man I am today. Without your wisdom, unconditional love and amazing guidance, I would not have seized the opportunity to learn the lessons shared in this book. I love you beyond words Mom.

Although I didn't end up with any of you beautiful women described within my book, *I love all of you individually.*

A Note To The Reader

Do not pass judgment on the experiences others share to help guide you. Instead, learn to pass along your wisdom with strength and encouragement to help resolve the very issues we complain of.

–Marala Scott

x

The Introduction

Why? That's the question I typically get at the end of a relationship. And by all elements of human emotion, I think it's a rather valid question. If I were unable to meet the appropriate standards, expectations or requirements in a relationship, I'd want to know the reason as well. However, the real question isn't *why*, so let's omit that from our vocabulary for the duration of this book. Let's focus on who, what, when and where.

Asking the right questions will provide you with the appropriate conclusion with less stress and an avenue to understanding your behavior from the other person's perspective. Part of the problem in relationships is that we don't consider the other persons viewpoint. And if you have, you may not think it's entirely accurate. Yet, it is how they see the situation and it is their opinion. You don't have to like it, but accept the opportunity to learn from it, change because of it, or understand that person simply didn't want to be in a committed relationship.

Let's begin by identifying more distinctly where the disconnection from the relationship came into play. Ask qualifying questions. Who was able to take your attention away from me? When did you lose interest? What have I done to cause your disinterest? Where do we begin in order to fix our relationship? You see, why, is too broad of a question. Let's get a little more specific so we can commence at the root of the problems and avoid the emotional blame passing question of *why*.

Have you ever had a man actually tell you how you can lose him? Generally speaking, men and women spend entirely too much time trying to deceive one another. The problem is that men will deceive you and when they're caught, they will continue with the lie or stop playing and end the relationship. Women have taken the same stance and will do the same. Unfortunately, because they are more emotionally invested than men, those strategies don't work quite the same and the results will most likely vary. Eventually, that road always comes to an abrupt end. The brakes have already given out so you'll crash full speed as opposed to coasting to a smooth stop. I'm tired of women crashing. Not only is it a painful experience for you, but it's an exhausting one for me. If someone finds gratification in your pain, they never loved you.

I've dated a broad spectrum of women, ranging from a variety of ethnicities. I'm twenty-eight years young, single and I don't have any children. Do I feel as though I've failed? No. Not in the least bit. Do I believe I should be settled down by now? At times I think it would be nice, but I haven't met the right woman. Until I do, I have no reason to settle. See, the problem is that I know my value and I know myself. I am honest about what I like and don't like so I can see it when it's in front of me and I call it with truth. Since some of the women I've met or dated didn't recognize their own distinct value, some have taken mine for granted or devalued theirs. Often, both men and women are unwilling to amend their personality prohibiting them from learning new things. Inevitably, they miss out on great opportunities and possibly, meaningful relationships.

For example, I enjoy spending time in my kitchen cooking delectable dishes for family as well as friends and myself. In particular, I take notice of a woman that loves to cook. I didn't say for me, but simply because she does. And if she doesn't cook, I'd appreciate the person I'm dating or interested in wanting to learn how, even if I teach her. It allows her to appreciate the time and effort I put into preparing a great meal for her, but more importantly, it allows us to share quality time in the kitchen cooking together and then having a romantic evening over a meal that *we* prepared.

Having the same interests provide opportunities to focus on one another in a more positive manner. It's better to have a cupful of laughter and perhaps a bit of lovemaking in the kitchen instead of unhealthy friction. Appreciating and sharing some of the same qualities removes the perception of it being a chore while adding the element of fun and romance.

I like to workout regularly and while it's been said that opposites attract, I prefer to date someone that is like-minded and has similar interest in several aspects. Sooner or later those opposite elements can damage the relationship and become weapons utilized to end it. Keep in mind that if she shares my interests I share hers, too. What people don't always consider with regards to relationships is after great sex, what's left? Let's see, there are bills, work, children, complaints and the rest of reality. That's why it's important to take time to make sure the relationship is about the two of you and not held together by irrelevant nonsense or a temporary adhesive.

Take a few moments to ask one another a few questions to help test your compatibility. You may be startled by what you learn about. Can you converse about politics or finances? Are you socially conscious and making a difference to impact the world? Do you enjoy traveling? Is your faith a priority? Do you want children? And if so, when and how many? Are you healthy or do you have impending issues? Do you enjoy working out? Do you like sports? Are you open to trying new things? How much of your time is spent with your family or friends? Are you willing to relocate? What are your career and personal goals? What are your fears?

What brought you together isn't necessarily the issue although, if under questionable circumstances such as infidelity, it should be. However, the real focus of a relationship will emerge with time when you have to put the work in to keep it functioning in a healthy and happy manner. Do you still like having sex as much as you did at the onset of the relationship? It's important to know whether or not you have enough in common to keep you together once you climb out of bed. Learn how to make a relationship work instead of making do with the remnants of what was.

My intent for writing this book is not to tell you how to make a relationship work, as I think we're all pretty accustomed to the fundamentals. My goal is to share real examples with you of how relationships *fail* causing a return to the single life.

We're always focused on trying to fix things for fear of failure, but only after the warnings become imminent. We get our oil changed after the light has been on rather than taking care of it when it's approaching the scheduled time. We go to the doctors when we've been sick for a while as opposed to doing what's necessary to prevent the illness.

What if I advised you to get your oil changed before the light came on or go to the doctors prior to your sickness becoming worse? I'm sure for some, this may be defying your ordinary logic so for the sake of argument, let's call the messages in this book preventive or cautionary measures. In order for this to make sense, you'll have to change your way of thinking and be open to a simplistic but different outlook on relationships. Having problems with your relationships is generally a symptom of something else. If you picked up this book, good move, because this is the first step to understanding why you're single.

Chapter One

The Catch

I spent the morning walking along the beach thinking about what makes a relationship work and subsequently my thinking shifted to what causes one to end. There was a point when I stopped walking, turned to face the ocean and allowed the tepid water to flush freely over my feet while I delved a little deeper into the curiosity of my thoughts. The sound of the ocean generously helped bring about the natural flow of waves in terms of my contemplations and reflections. I took a deep breath and continued walking leisurely along the shoreline as my recollections drifted in.

There are various stages in our life that allow us the opportunity to discover explicit lessons about people and the best way to navigate through convoluted situations we never thought we'd encounter. I've been there but at the time, the message wasn't clear because I wasn't ready to see it or there was too much going on for me to assess it properly. But I'm not the only one this happens to.

There are times when we see what we can handle, and that's all there is to it. The problem is that we need to be willing to see and accept reality so we can address it appropriately while learning from it. Occasionally, situations are comprised of things we need to experience while in others, we weren't mature enough or ready to comprehend the full scope of the manifestation. One of the most significant aspects of life is that we have the ability to learn from our mistakes, pain, or decisions every single day. We utilize the information as part of our educational plan for our future. If we don't, then we'll continue having that harsh lesson hit us again and again until we realize there is a developmental process attached to our experiences. Don't allow yourself to become broken before you decide to learn.

You might be asking yourself why *I'm* single. Well, that's easy. It's because I'm twenty-eight years old, I don't have any children, and I was raised to be quite self-sufficient. I love who I am, so I don't need a woman to complete me because I am whole. My faith in God makes my need for some things, that others deem necessary, inconsequential. Sure, when the time is right, I will be at another level, such as having a family, which will undoubtedly add an incredible layer of something beautiful to my life. But for now, I am complete.

Knowing who I am still requires me to work towards change or improvement because I'm not complacent. I am not afraid to go after what I want or fight for what is worth fighting for as comprehension, history and extraordinary lessons have made me resolute in my faith. I definitely want children one day, along with an intelligent, compassionate, fun, and beautiful wife. But until then, this is why *I'm* single.

I've worked hard to get to the point where I am now and I don't want or need to be recreated by anyone. After all, life is your journey to experience in the way you desire. Some people allow others to build them into something dissimilar to their true core, but not me. You can be whomever you want, just as I am working on the person I want to be. I'm not quite there yet, as I haven't achieved my goals at this age and I'm still a student of life working on my development. If that causes me to gravitate towards a woman in an untainted stream of fate as twin flames, so be it.

There are times people will try to shape you into what they want, but I've already designed my life according to God's plan so I'm good. I'm not saying I won't make anymore mistakes, but I am saying it is good to be confident, happy, and able to wait until I get exactly what I want or at least the woman that God places in my life because we're best for one another. Consider this, if she's with me, she'll get exactly what she wants too, because we'll have a high level of compatibility that will allow things to flow naturally.

I clean my own home and I'm unusually neat. I do my own laundry, drop off my dry cleaning and pay my own bills. When I go to the gym, I don't need you to spot me, yet working out together would be great. I love to cook and laughing–oh that's a must, because even with its nuisances, life is good. I never said I didn't want to be in a relationship; I just told you why I'm single and that equates to me knowing what *I* want. If I can let a woman go as easily as she came, it wasn't a relationship to begin with, it was a fling.

When I was younger, I had a great example of how a woman should treat a man. But for some reason, until I was mature, I took things for granted and didn't always appreciate nor respect the model of what I saw firsthand. I didn't apprehend that there were young women I'd met that had sincere intent behind their actions because they were exposed to positive and respectable role models just like I was. As I grew older, that sincerity seemed to become a bit of a rarity causing me to appreciate it even more when I saw or had it.

When a woman, roughly between the ages of eighteen to twenty-five, offers her heart along with her mind and body, sometimes, she hasn't been hurt or damaged by a man she once loved who cheated on her, was abusive, lied or broke her in some way. As they become a little older, sometimes the man or men that have done them wrong leave a scar on their heart or mind that is challenging or impossible to remove. This adds a harmful layer or burden prohibiting the relationship from working in the manner you both deserve. There are a lot of guys that have the same wound, which they prefer to leave open, making it difficult for a loving and committed woman to nurture them back to health. Bringing the past into the future means transporting your history with you instead of creating a new one.

The thought process of most women today is short-term. Women are so focused on getting a man that they overlook his authentic qualities whether they're good or bad. If you truly invest in the right man, your ROI or return on investment will be worth it. Anyone can catch a fish but after that initial euphoria of the catch wears off, it gets tossed right back into the ocean and his or her rod is cast, yet again, to simply catch another.

The first thing to reflect upon is your reason for wanting to be in a relationship. I mean, your true reason. Is it because you're lonely? Do you simply yearn for the intimacy aspect of the relationship? Are you insecure and unable to be by yourself? Do you want a serious relationship? Are you ready for marriage or children? Are most of your friends or family members in a relationship and you're tired of being the single one? Is it that you are broken and hope someone will fix you? Do you need financial support? Whatever the reason, take serious and honest consideration to identify what the purpose of finding that catch is. Otherwise, it's a complete waste of your time and will become a failing or sinking relationship before you have the opportunity to set sail together.

The roles are reversing and women are starting to find a thrill in catching and releasing a man, yet they talk negatively about them after the experience. If your intention was to catch a boy toy, well then, think about the quality of man or boy you were lusting after in the first place. He's probably not the one to take home to mom and dad for the holiday either. Once you identify what you really want from a man or your relationship, it will make the entire experience much more seamless.

If your desired catch is for the aspect of intimacy, it'll be enjoyable in the beginning but short-lived. Good sexual compatibility and physical attraction are easy to find. The hard part is everything else. Often, we get trapped in the sexual hemisphere and live in that façade for too long. Sex is sex and love is love. They are two completely different things. Sex is a physical action and love is a dominant emotion so don't wander into the realm of denial and confuse the two or you may get stuck there too long. When you come out, you still won't know what hit you.

I have several friends, both male and female, that tell me it's difficult to be single. They have an incessant *need* to be in a relationship regardless of whether or not it's healthy. If you're one of these people that can't stand being by yourself, the relationship has a higher ratio of not working out because you're blatantly and selfishly thinking about what you want instead of what is best for *both* parties involved. It doesn't matter if that person is a good fit or if the attraction is truly there because you'll make it work until the next one comes around. Understand that your behavior can help pave a dark avenue to infidelity. Discover who you are and learn to love that person because when you do, you won't waste time looking for someone to love you. If you can't find and love yourself, what do you think someone else is going to see? Eventually it will be the same thing you do and they will have the advantage in knowing precisely how to use you. Your lack of confidence is prominently displayed by a white flag causing manipulators to go after the easy catch.

One of the things people overlook is the value of the relationship and the reasons why it won't work. Make no mistake, the reasons will be clearly identifiable before it even begins, but you have to look closely in the mirror for this one. This type of individual will literally jump from one relationship to another so that he or she can keep the gap between relationships close. This alleviates them from having time to address their own insecurities. And if you think about it, this isn't a favorable position to be in.

What you're communicating is that you don't care about the type of person you have in the interim, as long as they keep you from coming to terms with yourself. If you opt to exercise self-respect it is capable of shielding the empty space where a deceptive kind of love would be. Respect yourself and an unshakable, authentic type of love will envelope you. Any *body* will bring you whatever problems they have and it won't be worth it.

There is nothing iniquitous with being ready for marriage. The issue surfaces when you're trying to *catch* a spouse or you're looking for marriage material. That alone can present the dilemma and create a disingenuous motive. You shouldn't search for someone to marry. Marriage is a serious commitment that's meant to persevere and that's another reason why I'm single. I haven't met the right woman to make that commitment with; at least, not yet. I'm not afraid of it, but I won't rush or force it. Allow that Sacrament to occur without force, manipulation, or deception. Let it happen naturally.

Marriage should be based on a solid friendship and built upon a strong foundation led by faith. If you're not ready to make the commitment, then don't. You're not on the clock to settle down unless you unnecessarily impose that demand on yourself. Don't trade your heart for anyone just to have someone.

Several of my friends are looking for a husband but a relationship worth having isn't built in a day. However, if you know what you want because you've been there enough, that helps, but don't search for it. You may be passing up the person that's just right for you or even your soul mate because you're busy searching in the wrong places. Allow a relationship time to be cultivated with care. Invest in learning as much as you can about one another, understanding that you'll never know everything. Knowing someone and paying attention to what you learn will give you insight to who they really are. Often, people tell you one thing, but if you look at the complete picture as well as the warning signs that came with it, you can see if they are someone else with a history that can devastate your future. Include something special like an AIDS test to make sure you're starting off right. Don't allow the relationship to be a mystery, especially if you have children.

I have several female friends that I hang out with and many of those friendships go back as far as middle school. I don't like to collect friends; I prefer to keep genuine people in my life. It's nice to go out, grab dinner and laugh about things or walk along the beach while catching up on the developments in our lives. Sometimes they offer advice and other times they ask for it. A common situation that I discuss with quite a few of them is how their friends are in happy, healthy and committed relationships, but they're having trouble sustaining a *healthy* relationship. *Don't compare your situation to that of someone else.*

First and foremost, I tell them not to assume that *all* of their friends are happy because in the course of writing this book, I found out that many women I spoke to or interviewed had serious problems of infidelity or abuse that they never disclosed to their family or friends. With the statistics for abused women being staggeringly high, how is it possible for so many women to be happy? And why do you think they end up in abusive relationships? Because they don't take time to get to know the other person.

There are several men who were victims of abuse. Instead of getting involved in an unhealthy situation, they should heed the same warnings as women. Again, take time to make sure the perception that someone allows you to see is his or her true reality. When you begin to see indicators or warning signs that something's wrong, do yourself a favor and let the catch go!

Secondly, people always want what they don't have until they get it. I always say I'm happily single because I enjoy it. Most people think I'm being facetious however, I've only been involved in a handful of relationships that appeared to have incredible merit. They were great while they lasted but sometimes it's good to let time pass as you may outgrow one another. Don't feel as though you're missing out because you're single; embrace it and use that time to discover more about yourself. Learn how to love yourself. Prior to committing to a relationship, you can teach the individual you're interested in your value. If they don't respect it, let them go.

Last, but not least, if it is your true intent to catch a man, then my advice to you is to practice patience. I have to remind myself of that all the time when it comes to women. Forcing something that's unnatural will only offer temporary placement, proving not to work well later. The right one will come along when the time is appropriate. Timing is important in everything we do. There's a reason we have stoplights. You know–the red, yellow and green lights that guide us. That light tells us when to go, yield and stop to keep us safe because it's not everyone's time to progress down that street.

Instead of putting your efforts into catching a man or woman, you should place your focus on making sure that you're happy with who you really are, not what you want others to believe. This way, you won't be caught and released when the right man or woman is soliciting a relationship with you.

Once you catch yourself in a meaningful relationship, don't think you can coast; the work begins from there. One of the reason's relationships have failed for me is because women become complacent. Once you catch that desired man, what are you going to do to keep him? If you were going to the gym five days a week, are you going to continue? You were going to church, is that no longer necessary? You were attentive to his needs and supportive in regards to his goals. Now that you're three months in, do you feel the same or more importantly, do you respond with the same enthusiasm or passion? All of us become complacent in a relationship but that's precisely when it begins to go awry. What attracted them to you and you to them is what is expected to continue while being appreciated. All I'm saying is to be mindful of what you did in the beginning to catch that person so that you don't come to an unhappy ending. If you begin to allow the effort you once put into your relationship to diminish with each season, well, this is why you're single.

Chapter Two

The Honeymoon

The definition of infatuation is the state of being carried away by unreasoned passion or love. Infatuation isn't solely indicative to dating or relationships. It can occur with new friendships or upon meeting someone in business, church or anywhere. The problem arises when you can't tell the difference between infatuation and a relationship built on substance. When you're in a state of infatuation, you won't realize it because you believe what you want until it backfires; then you'll see reality exactly the way it was initially presented.

The weather report said it was going to be a stormy afternoon but glancing out my window, I didn't see one solitary cloud in the sky. In fact, what I saw was the sun shinning as brightly as it had all week. I threw on a pair of sweatpants along with a charcoal t-shirt and headed out to pick up a few groceries. When I got to the store, I picked up a black hand basket and began shopping in the produce section, as usual. I grabbed some orange cherry tomatoes, radicchio, leaf lettuce and spinach, then placed it in my basket; but I still needed a red onion. I made an abrupt turn when I spotted them, nearly colliding into an absolutely gorgeous young lady. She had a smooth chocolate complexion and long, beautiful silky black hair. Standing about five-foot-eight, this perfectly sculpted woman looked like a runway model in the produce section of the local Farmers Market. She was wearing a cream-colored tank top with a blue and cream floral skirt hitting the top of her firm thighs. I was in a momentary trance when I saw her beautiful dark brown eyes rest upon me before ascending to meet mine. Her posture relaxed into a flirtatious position as she held her basket firmly with both hands and smiled invitingly. We locked eyes for a few seconds before I took notice of her ring finger to find it bare. I looked up to find a familiar face walk up behind her and toss a few small items in her basket. I observed a slight release of embarrassment glide across her face.

Since I'd seen the guy in passing before, I leaned in, firmly shook his hand, and properly introduced myself. That introduction provided the additional introduction to Ms. Lena. After small talk, I headed in the opposite direction and turned around to get one more glance at her only to catch her smiling at me, yet again. Naturally, I returned one and continued shopping.

A couple days later, I was responding to messages on Facebook and decided to check out my friend requests only to see none other than Ms. Lena from the Farmers Market. I accepted the invitation and gave a quick deliberation as to whether or not I'd initiate a conversation. After a twenty-second internal debate, I sent her a short message and ended it with my cell number.

Two days passed before I received a text message that read, "Hey! It's Lena from the grocery store. How are you?"

I really didn't know what to expect when I gave her my number but I was glad she used it. I began with insignificant small talk before making my way around to the only thing that mattered, which was whether or not the guy she was with was her boyfriend. And if not, did she have one? She responded and stated he was a close friend and that she had ended the relationship with her boyfriend a few months prior. After she explained what happened, all I could do was empathize with her. I could tell the sadness was still lingering, but she was stunning so I allowed the conversation to continue.

We spent over an hour texting back and fourth until she decided to call me. The more time I spent talking with Lena, the more intrigued I became. The best conversation to have is when it's not artificial or forced, and ours, well it just flowed as if we'd been friends for a long time.

We spoke over the phone during the course of three weeks before I decided to ask her out to dinner. She accepted my invitation and we went for sushi. It had been a while since I laughed as soulfully with a date the way I did with her. Typically, first dates can be embarrassingly awkward if the chemistry isn't present. When that happens, the only thing to determine is how to end it, but not this time. We had casual conversation about anything we wanted to discuss, without a trace of uncomfortable silence in the atmosphere. We connected on several levels, which was rare for me. Lena and I went on a few more dates and they all seemed to be uncomplicated. She was beautiful, funny and had an amazing personality so what else mattered?

After dating Lena for a few months, I came to a significant realization about her I should have paid attention to earlier. As gorgeous as she was, her extreme insecurities quickly became an easily identifiable drawback. It didn't take long before her insecurities constantly came into play. My infatuation with her radiant personality and beauty prolonged the honeymoon phase of the relationship, blocking my typically keen and innate intuition. I was almost a culprit of what I deemed to be one of the biggest wastes of time in any relationship. I mistook my infatuation for her, and clearly hers with me, as something that it never was and certainly not meant to be. The honeymoon was too great to step away from at the time so I overlooked what I inherently knew was present. I was complacent in my own oasis so I stayed until I realized the relationship was nothing more than an illusion.

Lena and I remained friends after I broke it off. In fact, we're still friends and it's been nearly four years. Each time we've spoken, she's been in a relationship with a new guy. She's steadily moving from one man to the next searching to find herself and happiness inside of someone else's world. I've mentioned it to her but I don't think she's as receptive to my advice being that it's coming from a guy she dated. She did admit that she tends to overlap relationships, but I don't think she's quite willing to do anything about it. Her insecurities eclipse her other beautiful qualities because they're a dominant part of her persona. They will hold Lena's happiness captive until she's able to accept the truth and respond with measurable change. Seeking a man or woman to validate your happiness renders you insecure as an individual. You don't want the foundation for your happiness to be built on someone else's property so they can have you evicted at any given time.

Women and men tend to live in the honeymoon phase, as it's the euphoric state that one dreads leaving. However, it's inevitable and the earlier you realize its over, the better off you'll be. This is when you will be able to commence building your relationship off of substance as opposed to an idea or temporary landing place. An idea is a thought that exists in ones mind. That's not a good place to stay while reality is taking place right in front of you.

Infatuation doesn't solely pertain to a physical attraction. One can be infatuated by the idea of love, also known as being a hopeless romantic. This is why the honeymoon stage can become somewhat drawn out. The idea of sheer fun and happiness without obstructions would appeal to anyone that isn't realistic about a relationship. Lena wasn't only infatuated with me but the idea of what we could have had together. I was a warm distraction. I didn't reach that awareness until after I ended our relationship. I was enjoying our time together but overlooking the warnings. She wanted to live in a state that was impossible to remain in forever because it was really nothing more than short-lived passion. As the novelty of the relationship began to wane, I attempted to determine what else we had besides the physical attraction and similarities in our humor.

As a woman, you have to realize that men need room to be men. Although we might be in that honeymoon phase with you, our friends don't care. The more you're able to respect the relationship a man has with his friends, provided they too are respectful of you, the better off you'll be. Okay, in the beginning it's cute to be with one another every single night, but think about the perception you're giving. He's known you for a month or two and he's putting friendships aside that he's had for a lifetime. Don't waste your time playing the isolation game because you won't win and it won't last. It's beneficial to be supportive of his friendships and interact in a positive and supportive manner. Guys have a bond that sometimes you can't break. It's not worth the risk to try if you really love him or want the relationship to work. If there are influences that aren't favorable and negative to your relationship, then they'll do you a favor and cause you to walk away or he'll end those relationships because he knows you are worth it. But if he doesn't, trust that you don't have the value in your relationship that you think. It isn't crucial to be a sports fan to connect or fit; just be yourself and let them get to know you. Embrace having a genuine intent to get to know his friends because that alone will go a long way if it's sincere. Holding him captive to your seduction early in the game isn't the smartest move and it's not a lasting one either.

This honeymoon phase shouldn't last more than a month at the longest. When you exceed this threshold, you're only drawing more attention to yourself. Keep in mind, some guys love that friction but sooner or later it will get too intense to withstand. Something or someone is going to meet the flames. The ball is in your court as the woman holds most of the control during this time, but it will dissipate. If you think you've won, do you really want to speculate if an underlying resentment is there? Although you want to be selfish with your newfound love, you have to realize that once this stint is over, you're back in the real world with friends whom you've neglected. Don't shoot yourself in the foot early by giving his friends or yours the satisfaction of being able to say that you kept him away from them intentionally because they won't respect your game. Once that opinion is formulated, it's difficult to reverse regardless of how amazing you truly are.

Another mistake to avoid is the introduction of parents in a stage that's premature. I've learned through experience that it's not worth introducing a woman to my mother or sister unless I honestly feel they have a special place with me or are a true friend. Parents are for meaningful friendships and relationships. If a woman asks me to meet their parents too early, I wouldn't decline, but I would feel rather awkward about it. I'd wonder why she would want me to meet her parents and feel that I'm being rushed to a commitment. Besides, it raises immediate red flags. Typically, when a woman does something over the top too quickly, she's trying to overcompensate for something she's lacking or trying not to reveal at that point, in hopes the parents and family will help encourage her new catch. I've always been guarded with women that want to introduce me to their parent's too soon and those that want to meet mine. Not okay.

I love you are three of the most powerful words you can say to someone. They can inspire, motivate and devastate. Again, this honeymoon stage is where infatuation and love are often misconstrued as one in the same. I implore you to bite your tongue if you feel the urge to tell a man you love him in your initial stage of the relationship. Love is often nothing more than a word used to entice the relationship to develop further. Sometimes it's used as a control tactic to gain someone's trust. Until you see consistent evidence that when "*I love you*" is said, the actions always match the words, it's not love. You'll know when it's love after going through a rough time. Pay close attention to how much the word is used when you're having financial difficulties or health issues.

Do I believe in love at first sight? I didn't when I was younger because I had to learn how to read people and understand what I was really viewing. Now that I'm older and a little wiser I absolutely believe, although I remain cautiously optimistic. I believe in falling in love, not searching for it. I'm a hopeless romantic at heart but I'm a realist too; understanding that love at first sight can still fall under the word infatuation. I found out that many people fall out of love after a vicious argument, finding out someone's not who they thought, or for any little reason including bad sex, just as easily as you thought you fell in. All I'm saying is, it's worth making sure that love is really love before you allow those words to soar out of your mouth with enthusiasm. What you may think is love, isn't. Sometimes it's best to enjoy the relationship for what it is without the expectations of hearing or saying those three words. Exercise patience because when you do say or hear them, you will value them so much more. And if you don't, you'll appreciate having waited. Those words can practically destroy a relationship solely because of the pressure they put on it. Before you use the word love, wait for that giddy or euphoric feeling to subside, as it eventually will, then reevaluate your true feelings.

Don't let your emotions run him away and be just as guarded if a man says it to you prematurely. How can someone love you if they don't know you? Well, perhaps they love what you have to offer them. The best thing anyone can do is wait until they're ready to say it after taking the appropriate time to see if you mean it. It's not about who says it first or how quickly the other person replies with the same three words, because none of that will matter if it's not real anyway. If someone won't say it, they're not ready or they don't love you!

If it takes time before you hear it, when it's said, you'll know he or she genuinely means it. Respect patience and the depth that those words carry. Throwing them around loosely will make us wonder how often you've said it. I'd want to know why you're trying to tie me down so quickly. Let us see it develop and feel it instead of telling us what you believe to be true.

Let the honeymoon happen after you get married. If you're too willing to fall in love without someone actually having to earn it and you can't determine the difference between love and infatuation, well, this is why you're single.

Chapter Three

Baggage

If you were taking a trip to a seasonally hot climate, would you pack an additional suitcase with your coat, boots and sweaters to drag through the airport and pay for another piece of luggage that you won't need? Well, the same concept is applicable to relationships. More often than not, if someone is bringing negative history into the relationship, you might want to reconsider. This is what's known as unnecessary baggage. It's something that is carried over from previous relationships and dumped directly into the new one because there's nowhere to hide it and no one else wants it. Both men and women are guilty of doing this. Regardless, no one wants to take over a messy situation that needs a lot of psychological work before they can understand you. Take time to minimize your baggage before you board your plane for your next destination. If you aren't able to deal with your luggage, you may want to consider your readiness and true availability to be in a serious relationship. You know what's in your baggage so sift through it before you take it with you. No one deserves or can handle some of those issues so the only person to give it to just might be God. Whatever your choice, get rid of it for your own benefit. People have the propensity to carry around a lot more pain than others are privy to. At times, full disclosure is necessary so they can better understand you and what they're going to be dealing with. Discard it or work through it, but don't hide it.

I was on the phone with Mom when a friend of mine, Steve, beeped in. I neglected to answer because he's one of those guys constantly reaching out in an attempt to set me up with one of his friends or solicit advice. He has a good spirit, is well established in his career and people genuinely like him. I continued my conversation with Mom. She asked if I had anyone special in my life or if I was dating seriously. The answer had been *no* over the past six months and at that point, remained the same.

"That's nice. I'd rather you remain single, selective and patient until you meet the right girl."

I took a sip of water and asked, "How are things with you Mom?"

"You know me, I'm blessed, which means I don't want for anything."

"Anything huh?"

She laughed and quickly added, "Well of course I'd love for you to come home but you're so busy now that you're out there in California following your journey."

We laughed because she's always out here on business and hanging out with me while following her journey. I make it a point to fly home and surprise her when I know she's missing me. Mom was always telling me to look at the big picture when it comes to people in general and be patient with my assessment. She says, "Everyone has a history and for some, it remains unseen until it escapes them. When it does, it may not be good." She was right.

After talking with Mom, I decided to call Steve back. He answered the phone sounding full of enthusiasm, leading me to believe he was up to something. "Dude, I found you the perfect girl. She's beautiful and looks kind of exotic the way you like them."

He caught me off guard with his statement so I retorted, "The way *I* like them? You make it sound as though she's a draft pick."

Steve laughed, claiming, "This one is different."

He was one of my most persuasive friends and typically able to make me consider his suggestions. For some reason, I wasn't convinced I should go this time. Regardless, I agreed to meet Steve and his friends out at a nice little spot the following evening.

By the time I got in from work, I was comfortable and relaxed. I really didn't want to go out again so I was trying to find a way to vacate my commitment. Steve had great intentions but his outcomes weren't always aligned with my preferences. I took off my tie and dress shirt then sprawled out across my bed releasing a long sigh. Fifteen minutes later, I decided to get up and take a shower before I ended up calling it a night and staying home.

I debated on whether or not to dress up a bit, but determined that I would go with a simple yet, casual look. I slipped into a pair of jeans, black V-neck T-shirt, Jordan's and a hint of cologne. It was a simple look for what I deemed to be a simple night given Steve's track record.

My best friend was unavailable that evening and I didn't want to inconvenience any of my other friends so I headed to Katsuya on my own. Securing a parking spot in front of the restaurant was typically difficult, but a meter became available right near the door. That never happened so I smiled, thinking the night was already looking up. When I stepped out my car, Steve eagerly greeted me, shaking his head as if he hit the jackpot for me. He began filling me in with whatever details he neglected to mention over the phone. I chuckled and nodded because at that point it didn't matter, I was already there and she was standing only a few feet away. We walked over and he introduced me to his girlfriend Mackenzie, the other couple, Jesse and Lara and finally, Ashley. Steve definitely didn't lie about her looks.

Ashley stood about five-foot-six and had beautiful green eyes. Her hair was long and black with a tint of burgundy that matched well against her tan complexion. She had a beautiful smile and perfect teeth. She was wearing a pair of blue leggings and a powder blue cashmere sweater, with four-inch stilettos, leaving everything to the imagination.

Ashley displayed a classy demeanor, which I consider an attractive characteristic. It was refreshing and completely captured my interest so I wanted to know more about her. After five minutes of conversation between the six of us, Ashley and I ventured comfortably into our own conversation. Fairly certain she wasn't a native Californian by her pronunciation of specific words, I asked where she was from. I believed she was from the Midwest and then she told me she was from a small town in Indiana and had been living in Los Angeles for the past nine years. She was a photographer for a high-end magazine and seemed to be doing well for herself. I glanced over at Steve and gave him the affirmation of approval. He accomplished something he had never done before, delivering what he described.

Before I left, Ashley and I exchanged numbers. She asked why she'd never seen me out and I told her that I didn't frequent L.A. too often, as I was a little more laid back and stayed home watching movies, cooking, writing or relaxing if I wasn't in the gym or playing ball. She smiled and said she liked that and was interested in finding out what spending time with me was like. I told her it was inexpensive and relaxing. When I noticed a sincere glimpse of interest, I invited her to join me some time.

Ashley and I dated for nearly three months without many rough patches. We enjoyed the beach, laughed more than most and cooked together often. To our friends and anyone that met us, we seemed perfect and for a while, it seemed that we were. The problem that evolved wasn't between us but I discovered her past had been living with us, every single day. Everyone has some type of history, but it's what you learn from it in addition to how you address it that shapes the rest of your life.

Once we expressed our love for one another, things began to go awry. As the months went by, I noticed subtle characteristics that were clear indicators that there was more to her than she had previously revealed. I began to look closely at what was wrong instead of crossing into denial and focusing on everything that was right. Upon taking a closer look, I had good reason to be concerned. It was obvious she hadn't shared with me what had broken her and sadly, she was still broken. Although *we* were happy together, I was able to discern that *she* wasn't happy. I had to find a way to open up dialogue and discuss it. At that point, I knew she would because I always gave her reason to trust me.

Finally, we sat down on the sofa and discussed the disconcerting details about her life. For hours, I listened to this beautiful woman pour out many of the tearful details that lead to her tormenting past. Our hands were loosely intertwined as she spoke with a nervous tremor in her voice. At twenty-two years old, she experienced an extremely traumatic situation that would be exceptionally scaring to any woman. The situation occurred while she was working with a trusted client. She hadn't come to terms with it, which was causing other emotional problems to reemerge and affect our relationship.

I could tell by the sadness in her eyes that she was expecting me to make a run for it and exit our relationship. I didn't ask her to tell me what was wrong so I could run; I wanted to help her. I reassured Ashley that what she endured was both heartbreaking and troubling because she was making the choice to carry it. She never told anyone, not even her mother. Regardless, I wasn't going anywhere. I wanted to support her however she felt I could. Judging by the expression on her face, she wasn't anticipating my response. I understood why the dysfunctional aspects of our relationship were present. Unfortunately, knowing the magnitude of her pain, I was sure they would remain for some time.

Our relationship was still in its first year at that time however; it never occurred to me that leaving her was the answer. I've always been more of a solution-oriented person, as I prefer to address issues head on so we can get to the resolution quicker.

What I didn't anticipate was that once things were out in the open, our relationship began to have more serious issues. There were clear signs her experience had caused substantial damage and she hadn't begun to heal. It even affected her ability to work without the looming fear. She refused to address what happened further and seek professional care, and I viewed her reaction to her flashbacks, as potentially devastating.

Several months slipped away void of any notable change and it felt like a warning. Since she was a victim of tragic circumstances, she expected me to understand, which I did. But I wasn't willing to ride the same fearful and emotional train she was on indefinitely. It wasn't healthy, happy or healing. It was difficult to watch her remain a victim. She was allowing the person that stripped her of her power, confidence and happiness to run her life, and ruin other aspects of it. He was notable in his profession and according to Ashley, never showed remorse.

Ashley's father passed when she was three and her mom raised her. She didn't want to add another layer of stress so she never told her mother what happened. Because she still worked in the industry, she didn't feel she had anywhere else to turn so she tried to bury it. Since trying to suppress pain instead of dealing with it doesn't work for long, *we* became a casualty of her past. As for the baggage Ashley carried, it remained tightly in her grasp.

Our relationship didn't last because her wall was so high that she never put her guard down or allowed me to ascend over it without fighting to keep me from seeing what was on the inside. Ashley rejected the notion of allowing me to help her maneuver beyond her painful memories, and work past the issues that developed because of them. If someone doesn't give you permission to help him or her, you can't. Love wasn't enough for us. The only person that can make the choice to reconcile negative emotions and heal is you. Many tried to help her and none were successful because she wasn't ready to let go of the pain. It was tattooed all over her heavy spirit.

Ashley wasn't willing to accept that someone could truly love her and understand her history. She isolated her pain as though no one else had a history, yet it is a part of life for all. The difference with me is because it happened year's prior, I wasn't willing to be submissive and allow someone I cared about to remain a victim and accept the consequences of their imprisoned life. She began to ignite her insecurities and consequently reveal more of what she had in the extra baggage she was lugging around. As time went on our compatibility dwindled. While it was amazing in the beginning, once love became a reality, she didn't know how to separate her past from her present and impending future. Our communication lost its luster regardless of how hard I tried. Eventually, we existed like an unhappy married couple trudging through the motions of a relationship.

Too much baggage can sabotage any relationship, as it's usually the underlying factor that both parties make the conscious choice not to address. Women typically compartmentalize their baggage in a negative manner and when it comes out, you have everything working against you. While baggage can most definitely be destructive, what you choose to do with it can change everything. Hiding behind it and utilizing it as an imaginary crutch to remain a victim or in pain isn't the solution.

Women have the tendency to hold onto baggage not mindful that they have the ability to ship it wherever they would like. There are plenty of guys that have trunks full of lies, pain and secrets that they'd rather hide. The best way to deal with it is head on with prayers and faith. If you need to talk to someone to work through your past, do it. It can only help you get a step closer to healing.

Everyone has a past but it's what you do with it that helps you grow as an individual. If you're open and honest about previous experiences but your significant other is unwilling to accept them as history, then you may want to reconsider. You could be wasting your time. Keep in mind; sometimes your past isn't something everyone can accept, so you have to respect his or her perspective. Don't fight what isn't natural.

The closer I got to Ashley, the more closed off she became. I finally hit my breaking point, which is why I ended the relationship. Neither of us wanted that, but we were delaying the inevitable.

It's imperative to embrace each other's past if you want the relationship to work. It's a part of your history but it doesn't have to be a part of you. Everyone has baggage, some positive and some negative. What you do with your baggage is entirely up to you. Some men, and even women, consider children to be baggage. If that's the case, you need to be cognizant of the type of person you're dating. Having children is a blessing and something that you should embrace and be proud of. On the contrary, if you've had an unfavorable previous relationship, due to cheating, verbal or physical abuse, that's the type of baggage you leave on a permanent vacation. Your baggage shouldn't define you. Instead, allow it to refine you and make you more resilient and wiser. If you're unwilling to take back your power and let go of the negativity that tormented you in the past, well, this is why you're single.

Chapter Four

Trust Issues

Whether you want to admit it or not, at one point or another we've all lied. The real question is how elaborate was it? A relationship of any sort should be built primarily on trust. Once that trust is broken, it's rather hard to redeem credibility in the relationship because it's never quite the same. How can you regain trust from someone that looked you in your eyes and disrespectfully insulted you by lying? It's definitely challenging since it's essential to have trust, but once broken, nearly impossible to regain.

I've lied to women in the past for various reasons and at that time, I believed them to be justified. Fortunately, with maturity and life lessons, I've realized that a lie is a lie having no shades of gray. The only intention and outcome a lie has is to deceive someone, which will bring hurt and destroy even long-standing trust. While I've lied to keep from hurting a woman, it wasn't worth it because in the end, the disappointment I caused was worse than being honest would have been. There were times I lied with the intent and anticipation that the woman I was involved with would find out and want nothing to do with me. That was my easy way out of the relationship but as time passed, I realized that wasn't the right way to handle the situation. Whatever my intention was, a lie always had the opposing outcome and it didn't make me feel any better or look too good either. It wasn't worth damaging my reputation, disappointing anyone or allowing my internal moral compass to go askew.

That afternoon, I finished playing a few highly competitive games of basketball with my boys for over two hours and then worked out for over an hour. Exhausted, I sat on the bench drenched in sweat to recuperate. After a shower, I planned on heading over to Midori Sushi for lunch. I was about to pull away from the gym when my phone vibrated. I picked up my phone and saw I had five missed calls and sixteen unread text messages, seven of which were from my girl. Most of them were in all caps but the last one read, "CALL ME NOW!" I knew exactly what the issue was and I was trying to decide how to handle it. I needed to make a quick decision and either buy into the argument that she was about to instigate or casually sidestep it.

I went home for a friend's birthday and ran into an ex-girlfriend at a club. My best friend, who's like my brother, snapped a candid photo of us talking in a harmless banter. She was in a relationship at the time so I thought nothing of it. When I returned home, I posted five photos from that evening online and she was in one of them.

I decided to call my girl and determine which way I should take the conversation since I was prepared for whatever came. When she answered, I could hear the distress in her voice indicating she was clearly upset. Instead of adding fuel to the fire I decided to handle the situation delicately. I told Jess that I knew why she was upset and that although I didn't agree with it, she was entitled to her feelings.

Jess was expecting an argument and I could tell she was surprised I wasn't giving it to her. I preferred avoiding arguments rather than engaging in or lying to temporarily diffuse it. I knew if I didn't address it properly, the conversation would resurface again to provoke an argument. Effective communication is key and it's difficult to do that when you're too busy trying to win the battle. This wasn't the first time Jess had been upset about something I deemed rather miniscule and I knew it wouldn't be the last. Being that we weren't in a committed relationship with titles and boundaries, I didn't feel she had a right to be as vociferous as she had been in other situations. We had only gone out a few times. Abruptly, she became exhausting with her mounting accusations and insecurities. Once a relationship begins to feel like a chore or a constant problem, if you can't correct the issues, you need to rectify the situation with a definitive resolution.

I explained to Jess that I generally remained friends with most of the women I'd dated or been in a committed relationship with. I never really had a bad break up, just compatibility issues that we were insightful enough to distinguish early on. Thankfully, our decisions have allowed me to remain friends with some pretty amazing women. Jess felt that I shouldn't be in contact with anyone I had a previous relationship with, but I didn't agree. Of course there are boundaries that need to be reestablished but only when the time is right and if a situation warrants it.

Jess didn't necessarily have issues with the friendships I maintained with these women. The problem was that she had an underlying trust issue from a previous relationship. Her ex-boyfriend cheated on her with his ex-girlfriend on multiple occasions and continually lied to her about it. I was being hit with the aftermath. This was the reason I decided that even if I thought the truth would hurt; I'd always be honest with her. Although initially she claimed to respect and love this attribute, she wasn't able to handle my honesty when it was offered. Regrettably, I ended it with her because the emotional roller coaster wasn't healthy for either of us. Besides, she wasn't ready for the honesty that a relationship demands and then wondered why guys lie. Wanting to know the truth just to fight about it isn't healthy or productive. Obviously lying isn't right, but don't add so much pressure when it comes to discussing the truth, that to avoid it, a lie is told. People make mistakes but if you allow them to be honest and hold themselves accountable for their actions, honest conversations will ensue along with the opportunity for healthy solutions.

Dating a woman with trust issues is enough to put anyone over the edge. As difficult as it may seem, you have to give us a fair chance. We have to start from an even and balanced playing field, no different than what the *first* guy was given. If we're starting from a negative before we've had a chance to build anything, then the relationship is a lost cause. If you have reasons you can't begin a relationship with trust, it's simple, you shouldn't involve yourself. It's unfair if you're making a man fight to earn your trust when he's done nothing wrong and you aren't going to offer it anyway. It's important to begin a relationship with a clear and level head leaving your pain, anger and mistrust far behind. Take wisdom from the lessons learned and utilize them if it becomes necessary. If you're unwilling or simply not ready to do this, then wait before you make a *conditional commitment.*

Most of the men I've spoken to believe that trust issues derive from negative previous relationships or marriages yet, that's not always the case. Women can lose trust from friendships that go awry as well as the lack of parental guidance, which may not have been exhibited appropriately. A lack of a respectable father figure can cause trust issues to develop with men and destruction to invade relationships. Before she's had the opportunity to place trust in a man her perspective is skewed.

Trust is one of the most difficult things to build and the easiest to destroy, especially with something so minuscule as an effortless white lie. Men need to be wary of the type of women they date, taking under consideration the type of past experiences they've encountered in other relationships. And ladies, you must be more prudent with men. You only know what he's told you so pay attention to his baggage because it's not *entirely* invisible.

It's imperative to take your time in the beginning of the relationship before diving in. Get to know him or her and ask additional questions that help you know who you're dealing with. When was your last relationship? Why did it end? Have you ever been cheated on? Have you ever hit a woman? Do you have a record? And, I'm not talking music. If you're not taking the appropriate measures to leave your past where it belongs and understand where you're headed with your next relationship, that's a problem. Do yourself a favor and deal with your trust issues before you transfer them to something that could have been good, great or pure love. You never know what the future has in store so don't cloud it with masses of negativity.

The reality is that many of us are afraid of being alone but this shouldn't be the case. In order to be with the one you love you must first trust and love yourself. If you don't, make an investment in yourself and begin that process first because the end result is worth it. Once you love yourself you won't allow anyone to strip you of it. If you're unable to do that just yet, well, this is why you're single.

Chapter Five

Baby Steps

As with everything in life, there are steps that need to be taken in order to achieve a specific goal. The same is applicable with relationships. Some women, and men for that matter, like to dive right in with their heart first. There's always an exception to any rule but generally speaking, that's the recipe for a disaster.

I believe there should be three different stages prior to entering a relationship. The time period for each stage can vary as every situation is unique, but the stages themselves should never be skipped. You can't go from kindergarten to fifth grade overnight so learn as much as you can. You need to experience your naptime, snack time and storytelling. After all, that's the best part of kindergarten. Life is full of lessons but if you decide to skip them or avoid learning, pain may be a recurring part of your existence.

I needed to get ready for work so I took the last bite of my omelet and finished my orange juice. It didn't matter what time I woke up; I made sure I had breakfast. I rinsed and then loaded my dishes in the dishwasher, took a shower and got dressed. I picked up my keys and grabbed my phone before heading out the door. The phone vibrated twice so I glanced down and read the text from Serita and smiled. It read, "It's your turn to come over tonight. I can't wait to see you." After that message I had the notion Serita would intermittently occupy my mind throughout the day.

Serita and I met at a dinner party with mutual friends almost two weeks prior. Everything was moving along smooth and steady the way we both wanted. Other than when I needed to amend our plans, there wasn't any stress or expectations between us, just great company and conversation.

My day sailed by as expected and when I looked down at my watch, it was already seven-twenty. I was engrossed in my work and didn't realize I should have already left. I had a habit of doing that with things I enjoyed. I was working on a project that challenged me in a good way, which was something Serita didn't approve of. I sent her a text stating I was on my way and asked if she wanted me to pick up something for dinner. She replied, "No, I just want you." She was always hitting me with something similar to what I'd say and all I could do was smile. Regardless, I was intrigued and wanted to see how things would unfold.

When I arrived at her beach home, Serita answered the door with a beautiful smile and nothing but a white t-shirt that read, "I'm ready," in big red letters. I felt uncomfortable because, I wasn't. I found her to be someone that I wanted to get to know but at that point, I barely knew anything about her and vice versa. I didn't know her middle name, if she had siblings, been to college, who her friends were or much else. Besides, I didn't know how many times she had worn that shirt before. What I did know was that Serita was extremely affectionate. When you meet someone you're interested in, getting to know him or her is more important then having sex.

The first and most logical stage of getting to know someone before a relationship is called *investigative communication,* as that is the discovery stage. As I stated previously, every situation is different. It's not until the latter two stages that you will begin fading out the unnecessary extras. From my personal experiences, this stage usually lasts a few weeks, if not shorter. Talking is simply getting to know some of the person's intricate characteristics and determining if you're compatible on those levels. You're literally talking to them and gaining as much information as you can before you shift to the next gear. Don't dwell on the time spent in this stage; just be sure that you adequately complete it so you can better understand your potential partner.

As expected, three days later I received a relatively long text from Serita expressing her feelings. She told me that I was amazing and fun but she felt that we were moving too slow. She explained that she wanted us to continue getting to know one another but at a much faster pace because talking was getting old and it would ruin everything that we were beginning to build. Sex hadn't occurred yet, not because I wasn't interested or she hadn't tried, but it was the easiest part of the relationship. I'd been there before. This time I wanted to know what the challenges would be prior to getting involved in something that might be difficult to break off later.

Generally speaking, the initial time spent together is favorable but I wanted to go deeper into her life and learn more about her. Besides, her interest in rushing things along made me a little uneasy about her intentions. Even though we both enjoyed one another's company, sex just didn't seem prudent given I felt the substance behind it lacking. Meaning, that's all the relationship would probably amount to. I was convinced there was more that I needed to know about her and I was a bit thrown off that she didn't have an interest in knowing more about me. The few questions she'd ask were topical and meaningless to understanding who I am.

What happens when you get involved with someone on a sexual level and pregnancy occurs? Did you take time to discuss if you were ready for children? Did either of you want children? If so, did you mean at that point? Are you financially prepared? Who will cover insurance for the child? What religion are you? What about protection? Did you discuss what you were going to do to make sure it didn't happen? Were you concerned enough to request an AIDS test or did you take their word for it? Talking is necessary and can bring focus to pertinent issues you may have overlooked. Are there other children involved? Are there health concerns that haven't been discussed? Talking can keep you from making a major mistake and if you're not seeking a meaningful relationship, then Serita's t-shirt works just fine!

I realized that spending time with Serita so quickly left the wrong impression. I didn't want sex; I wanted to get to know her. As you grow older and a little wiser, you will become acquainted with what you desire. More importantly, you will want to recognize the significance of choices that are necessary to have a healthy and happy future. If your choice is fun and casual sex, that gamble could come with a hefty price. Hopefully, you will choose to develop into a person that is ready to cultivate a meaningful relationship with the right person. For that to happen it's best if you display the correct intent from the onset. If you become sexually involved with a woman too early, she may misconstrue the nature of the relationship or fall in love without really knowing you and your intentions. The same way women want us to invest in them; they need to invest in knowing who we truly are first. For some, if you don't give them what he or she wants, they may suspect that you're seeing someone else rather than believe that you sincerely want to know precisely who he or she is. Ultimately, that became the thought process with Serita.

There isn't an investment in getting to know you if sex is too easy. You're just a warm body and another number. The risk is that you don't know which number.

If you're compatible after talking, the next feasible step is to begin a *routine of interaction*. Dating is a stage that requires much more of your attention. If you were casually dating and juggling a few situations, you may want to end the other scenarios so you can properly focus on one; giving it your best opportunity to work. This is where you begin to study the person you're interested in and weigh the positives versus the negatives.

While creating your routine of interaction, you will begin to devote time more seriously, anticipating a return on your investment. Dating is supposed to be enjoyable, so you should keep this stage light and fun. If you begin arguing during this stage and it's not a healthy debate, that's an indication, it may not work. Don't over analyze it; just observe the facts.

Dating someone can last as long as you'd like, as there's no appropriate time limit. The purpose of this stage is to ascertain whether or not this is the person for you. Talking is the preliminary stage, dating is the semi-finals and the committed relationship is the championship, especially if it turns into something permanent. Every stage is equally important in order to achieve the best end result, which most of the people I've surveyed, consider marriage. When you get to know someone properly and invest in the relationship in a healthy manner, you'll love what it produces. Once you know you're interested in that person, be honest with whomever else you were seeing and let them go, respectfully. Honesty is the foundation of any relationship, so be sure to sustain it. If you're not honest to begin with, don't expect it to turn into a loving and trusting relationship later. Besides, it won't happen without God being a significant part of the relationship.

Here you are in a committed relationship. This is what some men or women aspire to obtain after the dating stage. Any games should have been tossed out the window. At this juncture, you're making a conscious decision to be monogamous, give your all to one person and look forward to experiencing whatever the future brings *together*. The analyzing should be over but remain vigilant because what you've seen is what the relationship should consist of. At times, something you've never observed may occur. If that happens, take it as a warning. If someone is on their best behavior until the relationship is serious and your lives are quite intertwined, don't ignore those signs.

It's human nature to let people form a favorable perception of you in the other stages to acquire the desired catch. It's up to you to make sure it's authentic. Hopefully what you love about that person is real. Sometimes it takes a while but it's good to see what someone is like when they're upset, dealing with adversity or family situations. Financial stability is something you want to discuss too. If it's not there just yet, it doesn't mean they or you won't get there, but you will want to observe their passion and work ethic. Ask questions about how finances, bank accounts and bills or expenses will be handled. All I can say is pay attention to the big picture when intertwining your life.

I've witnessed many of my friends become involved in complicated relationships having completely unrealistic expectations. When they need help, they give their attention to outside influences that don't have the credibility, good intent, or a healthy track record to offer advice. Still, they take it unreservedly. This is something I don't recommend because it's one of the worst things you can do in any relationship. Whatever problems you have, you should do your best to work through them *together*. This is a partnership and involving others isn't the prudent way to build a healthy relationship. Understand that whatever problems you're having, your outside influences will add their perspectives and personal opinions. This may have developed from their negative history that can attack your relationship. If you need guidance, go to a source that both of you trust such as your pastor and pray about it, *together*.

As with anything, you have to start somewhere. A baby begins crawling, then evolves into taking cute baby steps, still fumbling, tripping and falling along the way from time to time. Eventually, the baby learns how to walk confidently and builds an innate confidence that allows him or her to do so without fear. A relationship isn't much different. You've gone through the appropriate channels to land yourself in the relationship so *be fearless*. After you learn the most important and qualifying answers that can help make it work, don't instigate problems. Work to bring out the best in one another. And if something doesn't seem right, it isn't. Don't be afraid to walk away. Remember to be fearless!

Relationships fail either because they weren't meant to be or you really didn't try to make it work. How bad do you want it? If both parties want the relationship equally as much, it's destined to succeed because you will both put the work in to make sure it does. Keep your negative friends and their tainted insight away from your relationship. When you encounter challenges, work through them as a team and it will help you learn to depend on one another in a crisis. If you want to cultivate a healthy relationship, always treat it as such. You may take baby steps in the beginning, but then, you'll know where to go from there. Relationships take an investment of time and trust. If you have a tendency or need for third party advice to intervene on every single disagreement, well, this is why you're single.

Chapter Six

Don't Settle

One of the easiest things someone can do in life is settle. You can choose to settle for mediocrity, an unnatural and unhealthy relationship, or a life filled with an unexplainable void. In essence, you can make a conscious decision to live a life full of happiness or one where you continuously lose. More often than not, we are inclined to settle for the easiest and most convenient outcome. It's human nature to want things immediately, as we're impulsive by nature. We see it and then our emotional craving for it kicks in. Would you rather take what you can get, aware of what threatens your outcome, or work for what you want unaware if it's truly attainable?

Personally, I don't want you to settle. If I were someone that sought after convenience and cared about public opinion, I would have been married years ago. Were they a bad catch because I chose not to settle? Of course not; I was bold enough to face the uncertainty that was in the back of my mind and respond accordingly. If I'm not absolutely confident about a relationship, I shouldn't carry that uncertainty into something ending with the vows, until death do us part. That's a life long commitment. At least, do your best to make it with the honest intention of keeping it. Consider the outcome it will have on both of your lives. More importantly, think about the longstanding affect that a failed marriage or long-term relationship will have on your children.

Denise and I were good friends for several years. She was a few years older than me and seemed to know exactly what she wanted out of a relationship, as many women do. Occasionally, we'd discuss our respective lives and relationship status. I was at a different stage in my life and unwilling to settle down. I knew in my heart, I wasn't ready for everything that came with the commitment and I didn't want to hurt anyone. At that point, dating was sufficient for me. I've always believed marriage to be a breathtaking decision that should derive out of love, not necessity. When it's rushed or forced, you are introducing the threat of risks into the relationship. Don't gamble on a decision you should make with complete conviction.

Years later, Denise called me and said that she wanted to fly out for a visit. I was lying in bed looking out my window, watching the sunset until one of my favorite shows, *Scandal,* came on. I was somewhat baffled because she had a steady boyfriend the past three years and for all intended purposes, seemed to be pretty happy. I asked if she was okay and she said she was fine but just needed to talk so I agreed to her visit. Denise was in a committed relationship and I played ball with her boyfriend when I was in college and considered him to be a pretty nice guy. She said she'd book a flight to come out a week later so I told her to let Dan know where she was going. I advised Denise to make sure he was okay with the visit and if he had concerns, to call me. Dan knew my character so I was confident he would be okay with it.

I was looking forward to seeing one of my friends since I hadn't seen her in a few years. I got out my car to pick her up and swung her around, no different than always. We grabbed dinner before I planned to drop her off at her hotel. Everything seemed normal, as if I had just seen her yesterday. But on the drive to her hotel, I noticed her staring out the window followed by a moment of silence. I looked over and asked if she was okay and she told me she wasn't. Denise said she was getting married and then a few tears dropped down her cheek.

I wasn't as surprised as she thought I would have been. I expected to hear those words from Denise because I knew marriage was inevitable for her. I was shocked that she appeared sad. Was she settling? She'd been with Dan for over three years. Based on what she shared, I thought they were progressing fairly well. I didn't understand what was causing her tears. We'd spoken once or twice every few months and after talking with both of them I thought I was abreast of their situation. Sure, they had a number of minor issues and disagreements but what couple doesn't? One was an ongoing issue that never seemed to change. If she was willing to settle then there must have been something good she saw in Dan that outweighed everything else.

Denise admitted that she loved him but was unsure about marriage. I thought she might have been a little nervous about getting married. However, by the time I pulled up to her hotel she said she didn't know if they were right for one another. I told her that whether or not she decided to go through with the marriage, that was a decision I wasn't going to help her make. However, I advised her not to settle because if she did, that meant Dan was settling too. Sooner or later they would have to come to terms with the issues they were avoiding.

Denise ended up marrying Dan nearly six months later opting for impermanent happiness. I refused to tell her what to do or give her advice to affect her feelings or their marriage because I knew she would marry him regardless. The fact that it was weighing heavily on her heart let me know their marriage wouldn't last. I felt she needed to remain single until the man that stole her heart made sure she never thought twice about being without him. Clearly, Dan wasn't that man.

Denise accepted the challenge to settle for convenience as opposed to trusting her intuitive sense. When you go against your intuition, you are setting yourself up to have your heart broken.

They filed for divorce prior to their first anniversary. It was an inevitable outcome although I don't think anyone predicted it would happen that soon. I considered it to be unfortunate, as all I've ever wanted for the both of them was happiness. More than likely, they both settled because they weren't honest about their apprehensions or true feelings. Dan once confided in me that he wanted to marry Denise because he loved her and thought she was the perfect woman to have children with. Somewhere their perception of the relationship got lost in translation. Denise told me she didn't want children.

To settle is to put in order, arrange or fix definitely as desired. While that may sound more than adequate, when it comes to a relationship, arranging and or fixing something is typically temporary. What you settle for is what you are more than likely stuck with for the duration of your relationship. If you don't like what you have before settling, understand it doesn't typically get better without an investment of work and sometimes, heartache. Relationships are about compromising. If you are not willing to compromise, then you are left with no other recourse than to settle for their shortcomings. When you make a commitment to get married you're signing an unwritten agreement stating both parties accept the other. Don't expect to change them down the line because that's not how it works. You can't change someone else. You can make changes to yourself but the choice to change belongs to him or her, not you.

I've always told my friends to make a pro and con list when it comes to dating or getting serious with someone. This list isn't necessarily for them to see which side outweighs the other. It's for them to visually look at the things they don't care for in their partner and see if they are willing to compromise on those specific deficiencies. Being able to accept your partners' shortcomings is different than settling. This is a common misconception when it comes to relationships. You can't and shouldn't plan on changing the person you choose to be with. Accept them for who they are and be willing to live with the choice you've made or let them go. My advice is; don't settle unless the only thing you are settling for is nothing less than true, healthy and unconditional love.

When you settle for something or someone, it's due to fear of the unknown. People have a proclivity to settle for many reasons. One of them is because they aren't satisfied with the person they are and they don't expect themselves to do any better. Therefore, they hold onto what they feel is the best catch they can get. Secondly, they don't like to be alone, so they would rather settle than be by themselves. Either way, you have to love yourself. Otherwise, you will always settle for less than you deserve. Once you come to terms with yourself and realize your self-worth, you will never settle again.

In order to do this, put your fear aside and be by yourself for a while. You should determine why you're afraid of being alone. What is it about yourself that you don't like? Understand these things and then work to correct the issues or find a good therapist to help you. If you decide to settle instead of learning and demanding your value you may find yourself back in the pond, and this is why you're single.

Chapter Seven

You Have The Right

Would you allow a random stranger to walk up and slap you in the face without having any cause to do so? Of course you wouldn't. As absurd as that sounds it's completely relative to relationships. All too often, we allow our partners to do things that are completely unacceptable when we have both the right and ability to stop it. You have the right not to take anything from anyone unless you make the choice to do so. Do not subject yourself to anything that isn't healthy for you. The option is ultimately yours so don't allow others to have this power over you. This, I have yet to figure out in a way that makes sense; giving your power away doesn't. It's difficult to find a valid explanation when it comes to love and relationships because sometimes there isn't one.

---◦≈◦⧓◦≈◦---

I glanced away from my laptop noticing a dense black blanket covering the sky as though a storm was rapidly approaching. I placed my phone on silent so I could prepare for a meeting the following day. Within moments, it started to light up and continued to do so. I picked it up to find I had five text messages and three missed calls from Sonya.

Sonya was an intelligent, fun and beautiful woman that brought joy and encouragement to everyone around her. For some reason when she was alone with me, she had an underlying sadness lingering about. When I'd ask her what was causing her bleak disposition, she didn't seem ready to divulge that information. We only went out on a few dates because I realized she had a complicated previous relationship that wasn't quite put to bed. We decided to remain friends while she figured out her best move.

I took off my glasses, sat them on the desk and rubbed my eyes before returning her call since I presumed it was important. Not once had she ever called or sent me a text repeatedly. Her phone rang once and she answered sounding quite distraught. In fact, I'd never heard Sonya sound so unwound. She took pride in maintaining control of her emotions. I asked what was wrong but she could barely formulate a complete sentence. In between her heavy sobs she kept attempting to apologize for her current state. I told her to stop apologizing and let me know what was going on. After a few minutes, she gained her composure and the crying subsided.

I'd grown uneasy in anticipation of what she had to say. I knew her aunt was sick and she had a couple of issues she was working to resolve, but I couldn't imagine what else it would be. I knew I needed to respond with a reassuring or uplifting response. Finally, after gathering her words she said that I was going to be disappointed in her and she began apologizing for even calling me. Sonya took a long pause, sighed and then told me that Eli hit her.

I'd seen them out a few times and didn't have any respect for this guy because of the way he treated her. At that point, it was worse because he crossed an invisible line. Once you lay your hands on a woman, you've lost what little empathy I could've potentially managed. There aren't any circumstances, regardless of how stressful or upsetting the situation is, that should facilitate a man ever laying his hands on a woman. Sonya began to cry again because she could hear how upset I was. My first question was, where is he? I wanted to go over to her house and show him what it's like to be hit by a man. Fortunately, my mothers ever calming voice of reason popped into my head making me opt against violence. It didn't appear that he cared about his consequences given what he did to Sonya, but I did. I had everything to lose.

I asked Sonya to head over to my moms house because I wanted my mother to speak with her. I told her I'd meet her within thirty-minutes. When it came to abuse, I didn't know anyone better for her to talk with. When I arrived at my mothers, Sonya was already in the driveway sitting in her car with her head on her steering wheel. When I parked, she jumped out and hugged me tightly burying her face in my chest.

Although I was extremely upset with what transpired, I had to tune out my emotional response because the choice was hers, not mine. Based on my own observations, I warned Sonya about him on several occasions but she continued to make excuses for him. Sonya had a right to choose her path, but she chose incorrectly. What I felt important was that she understood the ramifications and from that point, would make the choice to keep it from happening again. After talking with Mom, I was hopeful she would listen. I didn't want Sonya to think I was attempting to pass her off so I didn't have to deal with it. I knew it wasn't something I could prevent and abuse is not corrected or ended with more violence. We all have choices and inside of those choices is where our power lies. So, until she found her power, I sat on the sofa and reached for the remote to search for anything that would help tune out the painful conversation, although I could still hear it.

My mother spent about three hours calming her down and talking through Sonya's entire experience and relationship. She was identifying the indicators of an abuser and showing Sonya that those characteristics had been present for quite some time. After taking Sonya's broken body language under consideration, Mom and I weren't convinced that Sonya would activate the advice this time. Mom provided Sonya with options that would remove her from the situation with Eli.

After a few weeks, Eli won her over with the same line of apology Mom warned Sonya about. Sonya claimed that Eli promised to change and she remained in the relationship. Regardless, I did what I thought was best and attempted to help her find a solution instead of criticizing her for her choice. You can't fix everyone's problems but you can at least point them in the right direction and offer assistance. There was no better direction and instruction to come from anyone other than my mother as I've watched her help countless women over the years.

In the end, Sonya never filed a police report, got the restraining order or put Eli out of the house. She continued seeing him because according to her, they had too much history to release. I was disgusted and honestly never wanted to speak to her again. But I realized that the choice was ultimately hers and without the strength and courage to move on she would remain a victim. Empathy seeped in and I had to let it go. As bad as her situation was, the choice for change had to come from her. It was sad to see an intelligent and successful woman in her career make such a poor choice in her personal life. However, my mother advised me that her self-esteem had been broken into so many pieces that it would be difficult for her to believe she could walk away that time. But she said, when it happened again, and it would, she has loving words that will resonate inside of her and perhaps then, she will make a better choice. The problem is that many women don't get that next chance. All we could do for Sonya was pray.

I didn't understand how any woman could allow herself to remain subjected to that type of mistreatment. I empathized with women that didn't have anywhere to turn. What I had a hard time identifying with was a woman that had options but elected not to take them. Then, Mom explained their reality. I understand how domestic situations can arise but for the sake of their own safety and that of any children involved formulate a plan and leave. It may not be easy but it can be a life saving ending to abuse. I've educated myself more in regards to abuse and the emotional chains it has with its threats, rage, hate and sudden return to love. Women have to free themselves because no one else can do it for them. The same goes for men in abusive situations. Men are not exempt from abuse.

People have the propensity to take what is offered to them without knowing that their options are far from limited. You don't have to accept lying, using, cheating, selfishness, inappropriate sex, laziness or someone without faith, integrity, respect and strength. You have the choice to determine what you will and will not allow in *your* relationship. Be mindful of the type of treatment given to you and exercise that right to leave if necessary. Sometimes it takes you to make a difficult choice before the other person realizes what they were doing to you, although many just don't care. When someone is hurting you and you don't tell him or her, they may not have contemplated their actions. It's up to you to bring abusive and cowardly behavior to the forefront of the relationship and resolve it.

Remember that you are meant to live a life filled with love and happiness not pain and hate. While relationships are about compromising and granting concessions, it's equally important to remember to love yourself first and fight to sustain that self-love. It's not healthy to make everything about the man or woman in your life. You don't want to be the one that loses a little of yourself with each waking day only to find when you look in the mirror, you no longer recognize yourself. Your faded reflection won't lie. The choice is and always will be yours. If you're not willing to accept this right of freedom, and small responsibility to preserve, well, this is why you're single.

Chapter Eight

Define The Right You

We've all heard someone say, "They complete me," or "They're my better half." Do you really need someone to complete you? Shouldn't you be *whole* by yourself? Yes, it's absolutely amazing when you find someone to compliment your strengths and help develop your weaknesses but you should never need someone else to *make* you complete. It's not healthy nor is it cute to hear a woman say they feel incomplete. Confident men don't want to be in a relationship with someone that says they're already lacking. If you are helping someone overcome adversity and he or she evolves into a more positive and confident person because they are seeking it, well that's a different situation. Encouraging someone to be the best they can be is a good thing.

Defining the right you goes back to looking inward and being able and willing to exist by yourself. The best reflection is displayed when you're happy. What flaws do you have that need to be corrected? Everyone has something, but it's important to be cognizant of it in order to build a healthy relationship.

I've found the best way to begin a healthy relationship is to start with yourself. I'm always working on ways to improve myself whether it's in my career or personal life but the choice to be happy with who I am is mine so I take full responsibility for that journey. Focus on becoming confident so validation from others isn't necessary. You will realize that you're already complete and whole. Your faith in God can help bring that awareness to you.

Do you like who you are? If you're not right for you, how can you be right for someone else? If you're not happy with yourself, how do you intend on making someone else happy? These are simple, yet relevant questions that you need to ask yourself before you jump into any stage of a relationship.

It's not healthy to be critical of yourself; however, when your goal is to grow and mature as an individual, it's an absolute necessity to be cognizant of who you really are. Own your flaws and fix what you view as being a negative to a relationship or more importantly, to yourself. Ask yourself if you would be compelled to date the person staring back in the mirror. Often people expect so much of others; yet have low or mediocre expectations of themselves. It's time to change your mindset by transforming your thinking from ordinary to extraordinary because if you want someone that's complete, whole and healthy you will attract what you exude. Weak people have the tendency to attract weaker people so don't be one of them.

I was awakened by the sound of my phone around two in the morning. When I picked it up to turn it off, I had received two text messages. The first read, "Are you awake?" And the second stated, "I need you!" I planned on working out at five that morning and arriving to work by seven thirty, therefore, the answer was *I am now*. Before I was able to turn off my phone, two more text messages filtered through, which I had every intention of ignoring so I could drift back to sleep. I knew Kelly had been drinking and this was exactly why I took a break from her. By no means did I feel she had a drinking problem however, it was excessive at times. I knew she was doing this for attention but it was pushing me further away. Seconds later, my phone rang. As annoyed as I was, I decided to answer because I would never forgive myself if something happened to her and I had the ability to prevent it.

I asked her what was going on and if she was okay. She said she couldn't drive and was outside my house with four of her friends. I sat up in bed hoping this was a dream. Regrettably, it wasn't. My home phone rang and when I picked it up, my doorman confirmed that Kelly was outside. I hopped up, put on my Nike sandals, threw on a hat and made my way for the door. When I got downstairs she was standing outside and could barely walk up to me in a straight line. I shook my head and caught her as she stumbled towards me laughing and incoherently verbalizing how much she loved me. I scooped her up in my arms, walked over to the car and looked inside. I noticed two of her friends asleep in the backseat. I motioned for the driver to put the window down and asked him if he'd been drinking. After talking with him, I was relieved. He assured me that he was the designated driver and seemed as annoyed as I was.

I like to have a good time but that was rather embarrassing. My doorman was a replacement for the evening and didn't know me personally. Perception is often mistaken as reality and stepping onto the elevator, carrying a woman in Kelly's state, wasn't a good look. Once inside my place, I went into my guest bedroom, pulled out a t-shirt and pajama pants for her to change into while I got her a glass of water. Leaving her in the guest bedroom, I returned to my bed. I was beyond upset when I turned over and she was next to me. At that point, it was nearly three and I had two hours before I needed to get up.

Kelly was in a playful mood and kept trying to solicit sex. I gently moved her away several times before getting up and going into my other bedroom. I'd never slept with any woman in her state and she wasn't going to be the first. Granted, we had gone out seven or eight times prior to that night, but it felt uncomfortable.

When Kelly woke up, I was already gone. I went to the gym and made it to work a few minutes early. She called me around eleven stating she was really sorry for the intrusion. She wanted to take me to lunch and make it up to me. I said lunch sounded great but it wasn't necessary, however, I did want to talk with her.

We pulled up to Chaya's at the same time. She was stunning with her pixie-hairstyle, beautiful deep brown complexion and long slender legs. She flashed a gorgeous smile as we walked through the door. By the time we were seated at the corner table I requested for privacy, I already had the agenda laid out in my head. I had no intention of eating lunch or carrying our relationship any further. If all went as planned, she would understand my frustration and respect my decision. I've always felt that arguing is a complete waste of time. If you can communicate effectively both sides will be heard and perhaps learn something.

I asked Kelly if she wanted a cup of coffee or tea. She said she was fine and then asked me what I felt like having for lunch. I told her I wasn't hungry and just wanted to talk with her. She could tell by my tone that her attempt at apologizing wasn't going well. The expression on her face quickly faded from a smile to being distraught.

I leaned back in thought, rubbing the light stubble on my chin and determined how to address the problem. I cleared my throat and began.

"Can you recall what happened this morning?"

"Of course I can," she replied dismissively. "I remember everything. I called you didn't I?"

I decided not to waste any time and got straight to the question that mattered.

"Did we have sex this morning, Kelly?"

She looked at me and said, "I remember trying but you kept turning me down."

"So, you're positive we didn't sleep together?"

"Not really. I mean, I don't know."

I shook my head in disappointment watching her expression turn somber; she knew our conversation was headed downhill at an unbridled pace. She didn't know what else to say.

"How am I supposed to take you seriously or trust you if you can't remember what you do when you drink?"

Her line of reasoning was quite poor as she replied; "I know I'm safe when I'm with you."

"Regardless of how safe you felt; unaware of whether or not you had sex with me and not being able to remember isn't something to overlook. For the record, it doesn't make me exactly feel safe with you, if this can happen with anyone."

I told her that our break needed to remain permanent. That was something I didn't feel I would be able to ignore because it involved not only her wellbeing, but the trust between us. If she drank too much again and didn't get home responsibly, whom else might she be feeling safe with?

I knew in my heart Kelly wasn't intentionally that type of female. Nonetheless, it was the principle of the situation and that night, she was. It wasn't acceptable by any means, at least not to my standards. She promised to stop if it would change anything. I recommended that she focus on getting herself together and not for me. It wasn't a problem that she drank; it was how she carried herself when she did. This was the third time she told me she would stop drinking for me and to that point, she hadn't.

A few months later, Kelly requested a transfer with her company back home in Boston so she could be closer to her family. She explained that she needed time to regroup and think about the direction of her life along with her choices. Kelly's life was far from in shambles, but she needed to get it together and take better care of herself because a negative pattern was being established. Negative patterns are something that all of us have the ability to create and remain in if we don't address them. She was a talented and ambitious woman but she had distractions that held her attention better and caused her to drink as a reprieve.

About a year later, I was excited and genuinely happy when she called to let me know she was doing well. She resolved some of the issues in her life and stepped back long enough to analyze her behavior and make the appropriate changes. She explained that while her friends loved being out with her, no one ever told her she was constantly overdoing it.

Defining the right you means doing it for yourself. If you're changing your ways for someone else, it's disingenuous and won't garner the same outcome. Reflection can help you see who you are and contemplate where you need to be. Time alone can help you determine what it is that you need to work on. It may end up being what someone that knows you brought to your attention or it could be something entirely different. Regardless, the goal is to become a better you, for you.

When you define the right you, you're discovering more about yourself. It's not about being better for others; it's about you being more confident and healthy. You should love who wakes up every morning and smile when you see your reflection in the mirror. You should look forward to positively impacting someone else's life in a positive manner. Especially if it is the person you are dating or married to. There's already enough negativity out there so don't haul it into your relationship unnecessarily. Being healthy, focused and happy will allow you to continue to grow. You need to walk in a straight line before you take off running with someone else. Otherwise, they will be forced to carry your weight along with their own. Make no mistake that occasionally this may happen in a relationship but it shouldn't be a permanent arrangement.

At times, you can tell when a relationship is completely one-sided. A relationship is supposed to be a partnership. One of the best ways to ensure you pull your weight is take care of yourself by working to resolve problems instead of suppressing them. Find a non-threatening or comfortable environment to talk through issues so you can hear yourself and the truth of the situation. Be willing to listen and learn. Your well-being matters and you should always take precautions to protect yourself from harm. Irresponsible actions can facilitate enormous problems. If you don't care about the damage your recklessness can bring to the relationship, this is why you're single.

Chapter Nine

Entitlement

I don't understand why there are both men and women who expect much more from a relationship than they are willing to offer. I've noticed that people tend to have a sense of entitlement, which is completely unfounded. They expect the other person to pay for dinners, drinks, movie dates or trips that *they* initiate. I'm all about paying for whatever the occasion is as I feel a man is supposed to be the main provider in the relationship. However, a dual income is necessary to accommodate specific lifestyle desires if they exceed reality. For the most part, you should be able to take care of yourself before trying to merge everything you don't have.

What I find problematic are those that have outrageous expectations of someone, which they don't have of themselves. I love a woman that brings something other than sex to the relationship and I am quite sure that successful, independent and driven women prefer a man that can do the same. It will only make the relationship better especially given that financial issues can be one of the main causes of marital problems.

I don't mind a woman that's a few steps ahead of me or even a few behind, but their drive and passion must be in tact. They must have passion that isn't connected to mine and my passion should not be connected to theirs, for reasons of greed, entitlement or selfish purposes. Meaning, if my passion for something dies, theirs will too. It's not a requirement nor is it an expectation for someone to have material things and money to benefit me. If they have it, that's great but the other person should be able to accommodate their own lifestyle to the degree that will make them happy.

Additionally, I don't feel entitled to a certain caliber of women just because of my accomplishments or where I am in life. To feel entitled is to furnish with a right or claim to something. You have the right to offer what you're capable of. That's not to say you have to be an equal match to the person you're with, just have the same aspirations and work to attain what it is you expect. The entitlement doesn't always stem from the monetary and material side of things. Some women feel entitled to love, affection and the only piece of me that they would be able to break, yet they aren't willing to give the same of themselves.

I've dated women that were more accomplished than I as well as women that were not. There was a woman I dated that was financially secure due to her family's accomplishments, not her own. There's absolutely nothing wrong with being born into financial independence, except I feel as though you should still have your own goals and passion to pursue. She acted as though she had none. The amazing ideas she had, were nothing more than ideas. Her parents were more than willing to support and invest in them but she never followed through because she didn't have to. Quite frankly, she didn't need anything. She had her own house, a beautiful car and could get pretty much any guy she wanted. The onset of our relationship was pretty amazing. I did my best to support her ideas and encouraged her to want more for herself but that only pushed her away. The same way her dreams had gone astray, we did too. She wasn't interested in finding her own oasis, as she believed she was entitled to what her parents had already built.

Her feeling of entitlement wasn't necessarily geared towards me; it was in regards to her upbringing and the life her parents provided for her. She felt entitled to a certain caliber of lifestyle and wanted a man that could provide it. If they couldn't, she would, but it came with a price, dignity. I wasn't willing to sacrifice that so I had to let her go because I was taught to pursue any goal I had with passion, purpose along with a plan. I was quite content with my life and the accomplishments I was making. I was raised to write my own script and play the leading role in my life instead of in someone else's. What I provided her with was more than money could buy and she reminded me of that often. I had incontestable love that was carved out just for her but the material things appeared to mean more.

As that chapter ended, I remained concerned that she would continue having meaningless encounters with men until she realized it takes more than money to fulfill her side of a healthy and loving relationship. Money cannot create true love, as it is love that produces love. It was time to take my own advice and go back to the basics because our relationship was nothing more than a temporary illusion. After me, she dated a player in the NFL and after him, well ...

Some men and women are taught to go after status and money at a young age. In many cases, parents are responsible for some of the thwarted thinking their children have inherited. There is nothing wrong with parents providing well for their children and helping to create opportunities for them but they should never diminish their child's passion or pursuit of aspirations. In fact, they should do whatever they can to encourage it.

Some people want to be in a relationship for security. The only thing they may have to offer in return is debt, a good laugh and maybe great sex. People who feel entitled to things they aren't willing to achieve on their own can make you feel you're being used or demonstrate their ability to use others. If you are with someone that has that sense of entitlement, you haven't necessarily won the title of "Healthy Relationship" because when the benefits are gone, they will seek the next person to resume handling your job. It's good to be honest, direct and ask questions about the person you are dating. Determine who will pay, especially if their expectations exceed your budget. Be practical enough to save yourself wasted time and money.

I've come to know a plethora of women who work hard for everything they have. I feel their sense of entitlement to specific things comes with validity. What I'm speaking of is since they are successful; they have the right to want a man that is established or successful as well. And I believe men should be able to expect the same without judgment. I'm not suggesting that someone who hasn't reached their level of success isn't; I simply don't think they should feel entitled to spend yours freely. If anyone is comfortable being in a relationship with someone that doesn't have the ability to dine, shop, travel or live a lifestyle at their level, yet they want to share what they have, that's beautiful. When you don't want to work, aren't trying to progress, and make excuses but act as though you are entitled to what someone else has, that's a problem. That is a selfish mentality.

Knowing your value is one thing but targeting someone that has a value you can manipulate isn't respectable. What you do to others may return when it's least anticipated and *Karma*, well she might be the one to deliver it.

There is nothing sexier than a woman that doesn't need a man but wants a man. There is a world of difference and these women are in a class of their own. I've had several insightful conversations with men who say they want independent women. When she's making moves beyond your drive, don't become threatened and take it out on her. Allow her to inspire you to accomplish more. Put the work in and create your own.

You shouldn't be envious or feel entitled to take advantage of anyone's success. Become motivated by someone's achievements and use it as fuel for your own passion. Don't scheme to get what you can, especially if you don't love the other person.

Success is one thing but having a negative attitude is another. Feeling entitled to act any way you choose because of your success may be a detriment to the relationship. It's reassuring to know you don't need us and are completely capable of being self-sufficient. That alone provides another layer of security to a happy and healthy relationship. If your husband were to lose his job tomorrow, become sick or injured, would you be willing and able to support him and perhaps your children? Don't make success a competition or you may end up being the only one competing.

Many people express feelings of entitlement to a certain degree, but the reasons behind feeling entitled is what matters. A child may feel entitled to benefit from his or her parents' success. However, there comes a time to grow up and establish your own or at least, build upon what they have created. If a man is dating a woman that is successful in her own endeavors, he should not feel entitled to benefit from her labor or success. Keep in mind that when the roles are reversed, the same sense of respect should apply. If someone wants to do for you because it is their choice and they can afford it, then the solution is to show appreciation. Appreciation goes a lot further than entitlement.

Both men and women need to be realistic with expectations and be able to handle them independent of being in a relationship or having someone else do it for you. If your expectations heavily outweigh your own financial abilities and moral characteristics, well, this is why you're single.

Chapter Ten

The Grass Is Greener

The funny thing is when I was a kid, I was afraid of grass and anything green like leaves. I'd dance fearfully from one foot to another, trying to keep from standing on it as if something significant would happen. The race across the plush yard seemed entirely too far so I had no other recourse than to hop back and forth wearing a dire expression. Mom loves nature and she wasn't going to let me buy into *fear*. Until that fear dissipated we spent more time outside in the yard or at parks. I love returning home to Ohio, especially during the spring, summer and fall. I can't help but notice how vibrant the tree's and grass are because everything is greener than in Los Angeles. I always thought Ohio was beautiful but I couldn't wait to experience Los Angeles. As time passed, the incredible green landscaping is something that can't be replaced.

When you go car shopping, it's human nature to want the best car on the lot. In fact, you may want the latest model as soon as it comes out although you know it depreciates in value as quickly as you purchased it. The same is applicable to your cell phone. You already have the latest version and while it's less than six months old, you feel inclined to have the newest one and will do anything to get it. If it means paying full price for the phone or breaking your contract, it doesn't really matter because you're willing to do it. What is it about having something new that makes us feel good when we have it yet inadequate if we don't?

We live in a society where people take pride in having the latest and greatest of everything they can. This I know because I'm as guilty as anyone else. Now, let's transition this thinking into relationships. You've complained about all of your past relationships and how the men you've dated have been less than worthy of the experience with you. Some cheated, others were unappreciative and you've had your share of contemptible abusers. Still, you took what you could get. You finally have a man that treats you better than you've ever been treated and loves you the way a woman should be loved. He cooks for you, opens your car door, makes sure you walk on the inside of the street, pulls your chair out, remembers the most specific and intimate details of what you like. He is the epitome of a gentleman. He's financially responsible and offers a sense of security that you haven't felt since childhood. In essence, it is that man who reminded you of your value after others devalued you. You've even made the claim, with your girlfriends over drinks or during casual conversation that chivalry is dead. However, he is living proof that it still exists. Finally, you are in a healthy relationship filled with love. Women say there are no good men but we are here. If you don't see us, consider where you've been looking.

As time passes, your confidence has returned, which is great. Although you are happy, you feel you want to explore and find out what else you can get. This time, you aren't settling because this man is everything you've wanted. At any rate, you feel good about yourself and you want to see who else you can attract. Let's not mistake this new relationship as setting because it's not.

What caused your shift in thinking? Is everything you've been seeking and perhaps prayed for no longer enough? Since he helped you become conscious of your self-worth, you're feeling more confident and able to attract a better man. Is his repayment, betrayal? Okay, but just remember, the grass isn't always greener on the other side. You've been blessed with what you've been asking for and now you're willing to throw it away when there's no guarantee that you will find someone better or as good as what you have. Looking has the ability to lead to infidelity until you replace him. And if you can't, I guess he'll continue to make due.

The question to ask yourself is what are you *really* looking for? If all of your requests and requirements were fulfilled, what's causing you to search for something more? When you begin looking, you typically won't find it; the best relationships happen quite organically. Don't waste time hunting for another relationship if what you have is working. Finding a more attractive man, someone with more money, a higher social status, or better material assets is always possible. However, it's wise to remember that with every positive comes a big negative or perhaps a few of them. There will always be trade-offs, as perfection exists if you are accepting of yourself, otherwise, it's left to the eye of the beholder.

According to your initial requirements, what you have is perfect. What more do you honestly expect? Don't get ahead of yourself and be too unrealistic with your expectations. Sometimes people aren't entirely prepared for what they're asking for. Be sure that you're in the right frame of mind and consider the stage of your life, so you don't pass up the best opportunity you might ever receive. I've watched women stroll past these good guys and when they grab a bad one, they blame everything except their own choice. Guys do the same thing. They go after the girl they don't want to take home to mom while their best friend is the girl that's perfect for them. Open your eyes.

Ashley and her boyfriend were approaching fourteen months of dating. It seemed as though they were pretty serious when Martin asked her to marry him. I was excited for her because she had a long chain of bad relationships and some were abusive. She always prayed for a good man and well, Martin was that guy. Ashley had been broken so badly it was difficult to make her see her own beautiful attributes and ability to overcome her past, especially since it was behind her. Martin came along taking the time and proper care to build her back up with loving words followed by the actions to match until she appeared whole again. I thought they were perfect for one another. Ashley acknowledged that she never loved anyone the way she did him.

Martin was a Christian with an unfaltering relationship with God. He seemed too good to be true but he was exactly what he seemed to be, the guy most women *say* they want. He invested something in their relationship that most would not, time coupled with love. It took a lot of work to help Ashley love herself again. After getting to know Martin, Ashley's friends and family loved the guy. She said she couldn't believe her prayers had been answered. I'd met him on several occasions and told her, this was the type of healthy relationship she deserved to have because they were both happy.

I watched Ashley go from walking with her head down, to lifting it up, and then after her self-esteem returned, she became someone I never knew. She held her head so high that she couldn't see Martin. It wasn't that Martin was short because he was over six-feet tall. She couldn't see him after he bought her expensive clothing and a new car. She was looking past him, ready to move up to the next level. I warned her that she was making a mistake; yet, Ashley reminded me this was her life and she was entitled to having what she wanted. She smiled and advised me, "Sometimes you have to climb over that fence because that's where the grass is greener–on the other side, sweetheart." All I could do was shake my head because I was fairly certain her family and friends already knew how it would play out.

Without dragging out the familiar story, Martin was history once she ventured into another yard to play. The new guy put her in the same situation she was in prior to Martin. That's it. There isn't a happy ending to Ashley's story, at least not yet. Martin married a beautiful woman and went on with his life a few year's later. Ashley returned home to live with her father and sister hoping to find a job. The last time we spoke she was having a hard time getting back up. People have tried to help, myself included, but her spirit is broken because she is struggling and pregnant. It was sad to hear but the guy wanted nothing to do with her. Ashley said, although she thought he was better off than Martin, the guy was living off his family and unemployed. When they cut him off, things went bad.

Every so often, God will put someone in your path and that person is precisely who you prayed for. God answered your prayers and you threw the gift away thinking that person was your stepping stone to climb the fence and go find something better.

I surveyed men who confessed they took some incredible women for granted. Most of them said they regret it still. What I did find was that many of their scenarios were similar. When they were down or struggling it was a strong, loving woman that helped them regain their self-esteem and passion for life. Some said they were encouraged to try a different career that helped them get established, while others were inspired to go back to college or start their own business. Most of the men realized their actions were selfish or they displayed a lack of maturity and respect. A few of them felt they lost the love of their life.

Don't risk a good relationship for one that is speculative. At some point you need to understand what love, respect, morals, and faith really are. Like Ashley, you shouldn't have to return to the place your lesson originated and start over. Life is about progress.

It was approaching eleven that evening and I was sitting at my desk looking for a weekend getaway. Although Stacey had traveled extensively, she'd never been to New York. It was one place she wanted to visit. I found a package that seemed pretty good so I booked it without hesitation. I wanted to surprise her, as she often did the same for me.

By the time I glanced out my window overlooking the cityscape, darkness had collapsed across the sky leaving the lights from downtown all that illuminated it. Since the next day would prove to be quite demanding at work, I decided to call it a night. I closed my MacBook and plugged it in to recharge. My phone vibrated twice so I turned around, walked back over to my desk and grabbed it. I had a message from Stacey that had four dreaded words, "We need to talk." I had no idea what it was about but I decided to call since I'd used those words before. Stacey answered on the first ring. I asked her what was going on and if she was okay. She said she was fine but had been doing a lot of thinking about us. I asked her to be direct since I was calling it a night.

"I've been talking to my girls and came to the conclusion that, Aaron, you're just too nice. I'm kind of used to the *bad boy* type," she added with a soft giggle.

Stacey didn't sound confident that I was what she wanted. "That's understandable. I'll make your decision a bit easier, we're done." I could tell she was completely taken aback by my composed disposition because I wasn't bothered. You won't be when *you* know your value.

"Wait a minute. I'm not trying to break up or argue. I just want you to know how I feel."

"And that's good because I'm not trying to argue either; I'm simply being the supportive good guy. Since you sound confused, I want to help you be decisive. My time is valuable and I'm not an option."

I know my self-worth and won't jeopardize it to be something I'm not to satisfy a woman that doesn't know what she wants. Insecure men and women make the mistake of allowing someone they love to manipulate their emotions. I'm not willing to love a woman so much it hurts me because I was taught a long time ago that *love doesn't hurt*. And *you* shouldn't hurt either. I wished her the best of luck with whatever it was she was searching for, and advised her to be mindful of what a bad boy is. I wished her no ill will. That was the end. Click. No more static.

She called back twice and sent repeated text messages, but I never responded. Maybe this was the side of me she wanted? Stacey quickly realized that I was a grown man unwilling to play a "bad boy" for any woman.

I wasn't bitter or upset. I didn't have tolerance for anyone wasting my time, trying to change me or playing manipulative games. If Stacey needed a man to cheat on her, fight, argue, lie and neglect her, well, I wasn't the one. She voiced her opinion and I helped her take a definitive stance. I've never been one to drag something on that clearly didn't have a future. More importantly, no one should. If a man were to express those sentiments towards a woman, it's the beginning of emotional manipulation and you need to opt out upon the onset. What people don't realize is, you are the one that teaches people how to treat you. Learn your value before you begin dating so you don't allow someone to diminish it later.

I didn't talk to Stacey for months, not out of spite, I just moved on with life and presumed she would do the same. Eventually she did. I heard she was dating someone else but I didn't care to know much about him. If she was happy, that's all that really mattered to me. A few more months passed and I received a call from Stacey. I figured enough time had lapsed that it was harmless to take her call and see how life was going. When I answered the phone I heard sobbing. When she tried to talk, I could barely understand her. I hated hearing anyone I cared about overcome by pain for any reason. I did my best to calm her down. Finally, the sobs subsided and we were able to converse enough for me to ask if she needed to stop by so we could talk in person. She told me she was already outside my house because she didn't know whom else to go to.

About thirty seconds later, I heard a knock on the door. As soon as I opened it she fell against my chest and began crying all over again. Stacey kept apologizing for being such a mess but I told her it was fine. I led her over to my sofa and held her until she let the hurt pour out before calming down again. I went into the kitchen and made her a cup of tea. I didn't have to ask; I knew exactly what she liked. When I handed her the cup a few minutes later she smiled. Although her mascara streamed down her face, she was still as beautiful as ever. She said, "You always knew what I wanted and exactly how to make me feel better." I simply shrugged.

I asked her what was going on and why she was acting as though her life was in shambles. She explained that her career was going well but her relationship wasn't. Her new boyfriend cheated on her with her best friend of ten years and when she confronted him about it, he shoved her into a cabinet so hard that it bruised her back. When she showed me the bruise, it took everything in me not to be reactive. I took a deep breath and filtered out the anger trying to grab hold of me. Regardless of whether or not she was with me, it was difficult to digest the fact that a man would lay hands on a woman. It should never happen. I remained calm and listened to her scenario. She suspected something was going on between her boyfriend and best friend, but didn't want to accuse him prematurely. Earlier that day she acquired her undeniable evidence and wanted to confront him. I wanted to make a sly remark about her "bad boy" but chose to refrain from doing so because it was far from appropriate. I did advise her to file a report with the police while the bruise was showing.

She asked me why I was being so nice to her given our last conversation and the casual way I ended things. I told her that contrary to what she likes, this is how a nice guy acts towards the people he loves and cares about. It brought about a slight smile and then she began to laugh a little. I told her that I didn't feel we ended things on bad terms; I merely wanted her to have the space she needed to explore whatever options she felt necessary. She confessed that she felt completely at ease being with me.

After two cups of tea and a lot of Kleenex, she didn't want to talk about her situation anymore and transitioned to asking about work and my love life.

Specifically, Stacey wanted to know whether or not I was seeing anyone. I allowed the small talk to continue for a bit until she alluded to us trying again. I stopped that conversation before she came close to thinking she had another chance. I wasn't going backwards.

If you're content at home you're not peeking over the fence looking into other yards. Women need to think more about their own value instead of caring about how someone else is viewing them, your friends included. If you're happy, be happy and if your friends think you need something else, advise them not to live through you.

People often want what they can't have and then when they get it, they still aren't satisfied. While the grass may appear greener on the other side of the fence, you have no idea what type of fertilizer is being used, or better yet, the last time that grass received any rain. You should nurture the grass in your own backyard and stop worrying about what you're missing. If your grass is a beautiful, vibrant green, void of brown patches, then continue to help it grow. If you're reluctant to appreciate a good relationship and build upon what you have, well, this is why you're single.

This Is Why You're Single

Chapter Eleven

Capture His Heart

It's been said that the way to a man's heart is through his stomach. While that might be true for some, it's not that simple for me. I love cooking, particularly for women. It's a way to express love through, what I consider, art. Not to say I love every woman I cook for, but I enjoy preparing a meal for someone that appreciates the authenticity of it. I don't mind if a woman can't cook well, but as opposed to saying you don't cook, the effort is more appreciated than not making an attempt. I think cooking is one of the most intimate things you can do for someone.

Some think of sex as intimacy. While sex is an intimate act, I view intimacy as a close familiarity or friendship. And how do you get that? By allowing that person you are friends with or interested in to come closer to knowing the real you; not the perception of whom they think you are. If I'm cooking for you, know that genuine interest is there and I'm taking time to share a personal side of me.

When men are interested in a woman, most of us want to share other interests with them such as sports, business, family or anything that brings you closer to understanding who we are.

My passion for cooking specifically goes back to my mother. The only woman that ever cooked for me growing up was Mom. I didn't have grandmas, aunties or a huge family cooking for me, but I had Mom. When she cooked, it never seemed to be a chore. She approached cooking as an art and whatever she made–well, those that have had her cooking know it's the best! It was as if she were designing a meal that would be suitable to our individual palette. I noticed that Mom only cooked for those close to her heart as cooking is a passion of hers. It's the way she gives a little love to someone whether or not they know it. My sister and I love Mom's cooking and learned how to create with passion. So if a woman makes the effort to cook for me, regardless of how good it is, I take notice.

While cooking is important to me, food isn't the avenue to my heart; it's the effort. This is just one of a few approaches to connect with a man. If you go out of your way to determine his favorite foods and prepare them, it displays commitment or interest in knowing him on a deeper or more personal level. It's a way of demonstrating a willingness to go beyond the typical dating routine of dining out. Some women go to dinner and pretend they're going to pay, but ultimately she allows the man to do so. Although we go along with it, we can see through that strategy. It's a shallow way to attempt to use a man.

If a woman expects to win a man's heart for the right reasons or you want to attract any man worthy of yours, you have to be honest. Invest in getting to know him properly. The uniqueness of your creativity can be simplistic and fun, just allow it to be sincere. Whatever level you invest in is most likely what you'll get in return. Although that's my recommendation, make sure you yield to the warning signs that a guy isn't as interested in you as you'd like to believe. You can cook all you want or do whatever you think it takes, but if his effort isn't freely returned on a consistent basis, he'll keep taking what you offer but the genuine appreciation on his part isn't there. Let it go and use your kindness, loving demeanor and talents for someone that deserves it.

One of my closest friends from Miami, Janine, had planned on visiting me for quite some time. She had never been to California so that added another reason why she should visit. Actually, she'd never been on a plane and I thought it was particularly nice that she was eager to take her first flight to see me. Janine and l always had a special connection but we never crossed the invisible friendship barrier.

Janine often ventured out of her way to accomplish simple and heartfelt things for me. She knew I spent much of my free time writing and often asked how it was coming along. One day I received a package. When I opened it, I found a neatly bound leather journal with an encouraging scripture etched exquisitely on the cover along with my name. That's one example of her thoughtfulness and she did many things without expressing any expectations. Her kindheartedness caused me to appreciate her even more than I already had. Whether or not it was intentional, she definitely made herself noticeable. Any guy would have noticed Janine but this time I was more attentive to how genuinely beautiful her spirit was.

Whenever Janine and I spent time together, I'd always cook. Although I don't have any formal culinary training, I've earned the reputation of *Chef* amongst my friends. Some of them were just *a little* intimidated, so I'd always end up cooking. When Mom visits, I noticed she doesn't stop me from cooking. She always says, "No, you've got this," as she releases her beautiful smile.

Boldness claimed Janine one evening when she decided to take a few steps outside her comfort zone. I wasn't aware of her efforts until I returned from the gym and found her in my kitchen. Pots and pans were everywhere. Visibly shocked, I asked what she was doing. I told her, "I've only had my place for a year so please don't burn it down." She began laughing and blushed innocently. It wasn't long before by nostrils were enticed by a familiar smell. Before I could say another word, Janine told me to get out the kitchen because she was already nervous and definitely didn't want me to watch. I turned the corner and disappeared.

I was curious as to what came over Janine. She'd never attempted to cook for me before. Suddenly she was in my kitchen whipping up an extravagant dinner. I decided not to question her and simply enjoy her dinner.

I took a shower, dried off and got dressed. While she was cooking, I called Mom. I told her that Janine was cooking for me.

"I know," Mom admitted. "Be nice. The effort is more important than the taste. Don't critique her or make any clever remarks regardless of how it turns out because I know how silly you can be. Appreciate the sincerity of her effort."

I laughed and replied, "Of course. I won't critique her, but what's the occasion?"

"Why don't you think about that genius?" Mom said laughing before she hung up the phone.

Within the sphere of reality, it all made sense. Janine was interested in more than friendship while I merely considered her actions of a positive nature, not a solicitation to cross our invisible line. Whenever a woman does something nice for me I don't assume it's because they're interested in a personal relationship. I took the situation with Janine as a learning experience in itself. Perhaps on occasion I have overlooked some of the things women have done to display interest as a form of communicating their desires. The miscommunication transpires when we don't pick up on the subtle hints.

As apparent as they may seem to you, it's best to state it more clearly to us. When I thought about all the little things Janine had done, I realized that she had been communicating her interest, in her way, for quite some time. I always thought Janine was fun, beautiful and intelligent but I hadn't considered being in a relationship with her because we had been friends for so long it seemed as if our time had come and gone. Living on opposite sides of the country may have contributed to that outcome. It wasn't worth wasting her time or jeopardizing a great friendship. Janine knew how to capture a man's heart, but I believed that because of our schedules and distance, I'd only break hers and she was too special to me.

Janine didn't enjoy cooking because she was terrible at it. Prior to cooking for me, she didn't have the desire to learn either. I didn't care whether or not the meal turned out amazing or awful; it was her effort that I appreciated. In the end, her dinner was phenomenal because it was made with love and the genuine objective of making me happy. It meant more to me than she ever knew.

Capturing a man's heart is easier than you would presume when your intent and effort are genuine. Now capturing a woman's heart, that's an entire book in itself. For the most part, men aren't complicated when it comes to what it takes to make us happy. One thing to understand is that we want consistency in your efforts. We don't expect the world; we just want you to pay attention to the things we love, no different than the way you want us to treat you. We aren't always direct either, but if you're really into us, you will catch the delicate hints we offer as a way of not being too demanding or suggestive. As long as you are genuinely appreciated, venture outside of your comfort zone and do something for him that he loves. If it's football, learn the players on his favorite team so you can have something in common with him when he watches the game with his friends or by himself. If you're not the best cook, take a cooking class so you can surprise him and spice it up in the kitchen. If he works long hours every day, run him a bath and give him a massage every once in awhile. More importantly, just be happy and get rid of the stress in your life so you can focus on one another in a healthy manner. These are simple ways to capture and keep a man's heart.

I'm sure if you are investing in the person you're interested in, it's not for a temporary relationship. The investment doesn't mean financially because there are numerous ways to strengthen your bond. Going out of your way for someone is a great way sustain a relationship. Make it a point to have fun *together*. If you're not enthusiastic about extending yourself for a healthy and fun relationship, perhaps, this is why you're single.

Chapter Twelve

Lies

Trust is one of the hardest things to build in any type of relationship or friendship. It's something that isn't always gifted to you so be willing to earn it. As difficult as it is to build, it's ten times easier to break. Once it's broken, even if you're given the opportunity to gain it back, the relationship typically isn't quite the same. For this reason, don't put yourself in that predicament. Yes, the truth typically hurts but a lie cuts deep, as it exposes the truth about your character. If you choose to lie you are attempting to deceive the person you are supposed to love and trust. That's not the way to develop a healthy relationship and this is why *you're* single!

Chapter Thirteen

Moments vs. Milestones

Is an amazing moment or reaching a milestone more worthy of a celebration? Personally, I'm more apt to celebrate an incredible moment. You shouldn't need a reason to do something thoughtful for the person you love. If I send you flowers on a random Thursday afternoon, it should mean just as much, if not more, than sending you flowers on Valentine's Day. If I cooked you dinner Tuesday evening for no reason at all, does it not have the same value as cooking dinner for your birthday? All too often we put expectations on milestones that we may never have the opportunity of reaching. Change your way of thinking and live in the moment. Enjoy the happiness you have while it's there.

People celebrate milestones because they've defied the expectations that others have set on their relationship. In more simplistic terms, this means that your happiness is determined by fulfilling the requirements of others. When this happens, you're not living in the moment; you're living for someone else. Their happiness will never be aligned with yours, as everyone's happiness is unique to them. Essentially, you're merely chasing a dream. The future isn't promised to any of us, so it's important to cherish what you have, while you have it. I'm not saying you shouldn't plan, but don't overlook the beautiful love that you've created in a particular moment because you're expecting something better when you reach a milestone.

I woke up and stretched out my arms as the sun extended its rays, casting its light across my face. I reached for my phone to see if I had any new messages. I rarely went out, but found it amusing to check the drunken texts and missed calls I had from friends. I skimmed through some messages making a mental notation of what I would later respond to and then I saw Maya's. It read, "Good morning baby, happy six months!" I was surprised to find this message. While six months had significance to her, it was Saturday morning to me. I reluctantly responded with a similar text. I placed my phone on my nightstand and sat up wearing a look of confusion. Was I supposed to have something planned for that day?

Maya always reminded me when we met a particular milestone. When we hit three months, she let me know it was the longest relationship she'd had in nearly three years. This time, we were celebrating a six-month success. I found it odd that she felt compelled to express our success when achieving a certain milestone as if we were not expected to make it. I, on the other hand, was happy to take a walk along the beach. I enjoyed laughing with her and cuddling on the sofa with a soft throw tossed across her voluptuous frame. I didn't need to be with her for six months before I could celebrate the things I loved about her. Six months, three months or two weeks was all the same for me. I was living in the moment while she was highlighting the things she deemed to be an accomplishment in the relationship. It made me wonder how many of the little things she had overlooked while waiting for the bigger milestones. I favored the quality of our relationship over the duration of time we were together.

I had a handful of friends that were in a relationship where arguments seemed to ensue over every little thing. But when the one-year anniversary of dating arrived, they went out to dinner and celebrated with gifts. I didn't get it nor did I want to. Is it more important to be in an unhealthy relationship, lacking love and respect just to say you're in one? Does celebrating a milestone make the relationship stronger or better if the daily appreciation isn't present?

Maya consistently displayed her motivation for achieving mini milestones more than she did enjoying the daily beauty in our relationship. She was proud of herself for being in a committed and healthy relationship contrary to the not so affable experiences of her previous. I recognized this on our six-month anniversary. On that particular day, I left work early. I went to the store to pick up scallops, fresh spinach and potatoes so I could make her one of her favorite meals. I made a second stop to grab flowers, candles and a card. When I arrived, she answered the door and gave me a quick peck. She was dressed in her normal style of dress and nothing was out of the ordinary. I didn't have any expectations but I figured since she felt compelled to recognize that day as a milestone in our relationship, I should do something sweet for her. It didn't feel as exciting as it should have been, probably because it was something I preferred to do on random occasions. I don't find it natural when it feels like an assignment. Regardless, I carried on with that evening as intended.

The following day I went to see Maya and told her that we needed to talk. The previous day made me aware of the problem in our relationship. I thought she was an amazing woman but appeared uninhabited by authentic joy and satisfaction. Everything she did and every move she made was determined by the response or reaction of others towards her. She said she loved our relationship and her parents really liked me, as I wasn't her typical guy. She explained that she'd rather date someone steady as opposed to looking for love as she had continuously done in her past. Maya had some underlying issues and unfortunately wasn't able to let go of them. Reaching these milestones was giving her something to look forward to in our relationship. She loved the idea of us, but couldn't fully love me because she didn't love herself, yet. She thought the longer we stayed together was proof that our relationship was working. She was hoping I could teach her to love herself.

While I recognize the value of celebrating for a necessary or fun cause, I feel there is too much significance placed on specific holidays. We should be thankful for the beauty in every moment shared with that special person in your life. When celebrating holidays or milestones, allow someone to do it because they want to, not because the calendar or media is a reminder that it is an obligation. You can have a man that brings you flowers and gifts on Valentine's Day but he's cheating on you and gave them to his other three women too. What's the purpose again? If you have to force, remind or ask someone to celebrate a milestone, perhaps they aren't as connected to the relationship the way you are. The only thing that can come from it is disappointment. Accept and appreciate what is natural and heartfelt.

It's definitely essential to celebrate the mountains you've moved or climbed in any relationship. Celebrating someone's anniversary for being cancer free or more meaningful things is inspiring. However, it's just as important to enjoy what you have while you have it with that person. Do things when you feel compelled to. Own the moments and celebrate life by taking in every bit of joy and your milestones will be more appreciated with time. If you're always measuring, then how can you possibly enjoy your relationship? If you won't live in the moment and appreciate the gifts you have, this is why you're single.

.

Chapter Fourteen

Be A Priority

The definition of selfish is lacking consideration for others or being concerned chiefly with one's own personal profit or pleasure. While it may sound like something that should never occur in a relationship, there are certain instances where you can and should be a priority.

Relationships can be one-sided and not for lack of compromise but because one person is selfish. They are self-absorbed and concerned with their own happiness above and beyond anyone else. Therefore their selfishness is primarily for personal gain devoid of positive intent. This type of behavior is not what I'm referencing as acceptable.

Often, a breaking point will transcend in a relationship where someone comes to the realization that they are the only one putting in effort to make the relationship, not continue to exist, but work. When this transpires, one of two things is likely to occur. Someone will either emotionally check out and shut down or they will walk away from the relationship entirely. Neither one of these outcomes are a desired end result, yet it is inevitable for those unwilling to recognize their shortcomings. Being selfish in a relationship for the wrong reasons is rather damaging and can be emotionally abusive. You're showing your partner that you care more about yourself than what you are trying to build together. Being a priority and taking care of yourself will better allow you to have the energy, passion and focus to be there for others. You need to be happy.

It was late in the evening and I returned home from the studio. Though I should have been on my way to another destination, I wanted to grab a few moments of peace before heading back out to a dinner invitation. I sat down on my sofa, turned on the songs I had just recorded and allowed the music to flush through my soul. Whenever I have a chance to write or create, I dive into it locking everything else out, including time. I find it to be a liberating and therapeutic release of self-expression. Sometimes the lyrics flow from the deepest part of my subconscious quite unreservedly and the final result is amazing. I'd been surrounded by music my entire life and have been blessed with some incredible influences.

I leaned back and let out a heavy exhale thinking about some of the projects I was working on. Since I'd been in Los Angeles, I'd done some acting, a lot of music, a tremendous amount of writing and I still managed to have a great career. It didn't seem that I was resting enough and I could feel it. Being in pursuit of and accomplishing the things I love keeps me happy, progressing and feeling the presence of God with every move I make. But, it is God whom created the Sabbath day.

At times, I'm asked to help resolve problems for some of my friends that are going through a rough patch in their marriage or relationship. On other occasions, I'm pulled in many directions for diverse reasons.

My family is back home in Ohio and my time with them is valuable whether it's over the phone or in person. One of the things I love is that when I talk with either of them, they remind me to take care of myself. They are always advising me to get more rest and slow down. They know how much I go from one end of the day to the next, which is why they say to make myself a priority.

People really never know what's going on in your personal life making it easy for you to be pulled in all types of directions. But the key is learning when to say, *no*. It's important to trust your body when it's telling you that you're tired, your mind when it says your stressed, and your intuition when people don't care if you're last or not at all. Be a priority.

Having time to myself, listening to music and relaxing allowed me feel how exhausted I really was. When your body tells you to stop, stop. Learn to rest and take care of your health before running yourself into the ground. If no one can see that you've been working too much, running a little too hard, handling everyone else's problems and pulled in so many directions that you don't know which day it is, they don't care. So care about yourself.

I decided to stay home that evening and when I called Brett and Katrina to cancel, they completely understood. They didn't attempt to make me feel guilty or bad which is one of the reasons I appreciate their friendship. Had I not made myself a priority and gone home for an intermission I wouldn't have been good company anyway.

One of my close friends was in a one-sided relationship. For nearly a year, I've watched Megan continuously do the most heartfelt things for her boyfriend. Her intent was genuine and pure with the most simplistic of hopes, which was to keep him happy. She planned sentimental trips and did some rather nice things without any expectations other than for him to be happy. As an outsider looking in, I knew, without a doubt, that everything she did for Rob was out of the kindness of her heart. It pained me to see his feelings expressed an inequality because they weren't reciprocated in any fashion. She had done so much for him; it caused a financial burden for her. Rob didn't appreciate what he had in Megan nor did he return the sentiment. He just kept taking.

Part of their problem was that Megan was teaching him to be selfish. She was teaching Rob how to treat her while putting herself last in the process. She wasn't a priority to herself and definitely not one to Rob. If I've learned nothing else, I know with the exception of circumstances suggesting danger, you shouldn't intervene in a friend's relationship, unless they ask, and you recognize they're ready for the truth. Unfortunately, they have to make those choices so you aren't blamed later while their relationship remains unchanged.

As with many things in life, a relationship can be a bit of a gamble in certain aspects. If you're interested in someone, be open to learning things that you weren't told or didn't see initially. Additionally, be prepared to find out things about their past they either weren't ready or were not going to tell you. Typically the way you learn about the negative attributes a person has is out of the mouth of an angry ex or when the behavior slips out, causing you to take notice and then, question it. If someone is selfish, that's who he or she is. You can give and keep giving until you're depleted. That's why it is important to make yourself a priority, especially when you sense that your efforts, generosity or kindness isn't reciprocal.

In Megan's situation, it took approximately two years for her to accept that Rob wasn't the man for her. As their relationship crumbled, I gave her advice to take under consideration and provided the necessary support when she called me. I wanted Megan to open her mind and see how much she had neglected herself. I often advised her to begin making herself the priority, but she thought it would make her appear selfish. Nevertheless, I avoided overstepping my boundaries.

The last time I'd given Megan advice was prior to the complete collapse of her relationship. I let her know that it was okay to make yourself a priority. In addition, I advised her to invest in making herself happy. She wasn't exactly receptive to what I was saying so I gave her some recommendations. Given that she was a friend, I felt compelled to elaborate that time because she wasn't seeing it from an unbiased perspective. She believed if she stopped doing things, he wouldn't love her. From my perspective, I told her what she had wasn't love.

Since the beginning of her relationship, she compromised her beliefs and everything she stood for to please Rob. One day she was in a car accident and when she called him, although he wasn't working, he didn't go to the hospital. He didn't check on her until a week later.

She put everything she possibly could into their relationship and was given nothing in return other than a broken heart, poor self-esteem and debt. It was time for her to limit her accessibility and bountiful contributions to Rob. Megan needed to do the things she enjoyed and invest generously in herself. Megan needed to learn how to become a priority.

Rob was younger than Megan by six years. While that may have had something to do with his lack of maturity and their relationship overall, he was old enough to know that he wasn't investing in their relationship and Megan was giving everything she had. One day, Megan actually took my advice, put it into action and observed how quickly it began to work. It made Rob recognize how much she was doing for him and the first time she stopped, he questioned it. It didn't work to her advantage, but it made her see his selfishness more clearly. It was evident that he expected things to continue along the path she had established, but they didn't. Shortly after her transitional shift, he told her that he needed time to be by himself and then he broke it off with her.

If you're still unclear as to why you should be a priority, that's because you're not a selfish person. I view that as a great thing as long as you aren't the casualty. Things need to change if no one is making you the priority. Unfortunately, sometimes it's necessary, especially for those of us that are the givers, pleasers and doers in the relationship. Being a priority, if even for an instant, will help put a situation into perspective and you in a healthier mindset. For one, it will make you realize what you've been giving up and missing out on by neglecting to take care of yourself. Secondly, it will illuminate your situation and potentially help you realize how selfless you've been. If you're reluctant to become a priority for the sake of understanding your value, this is why you're single.

Chapter Fifteen

Get Out The Game

Being in a committed relationship isn't like playing an interminable yet calculated game of chess where every move is critical and vital to the end result. Playing the field is a rather intensive game that you must be willing to devote your time and attention to. It can move at a fleeting pace or be long and drawn out. If an intermittent relationship seems like a game, it usually is, just stop playing. When you want to give a relationship a real chance at being successful, you have to be willing to hang up the jersey and retire from playing the game. That's when loyalty and respect for the relationship will be set in motion.

In order to be great at any one thing, it's imperative to focus your efforts on whatever that particular thing is, until you master it. The same is applicable to a relationship. Until you're in a place where the loyalty, trust and your bond are unyielding, you shouldn't allow outsiders to impede your progress. There are situations when people sabotage your happiness. They don't want you to have what they don't. Don't allow others the ability to create opportunities that cause you to fight and question your relationship. If you see something wrong, you should be the one to address it or if it's detrimental to the relationship, end it.

If you are straddling the fence you're not fully committed, which makes it implausible to give your relationship a fair shot. Until you've made that lifelong commitment, known as marriage, your attention needs to be focused on the person in front of you if you truly want a future with them. If you're still looking around and soliciting options, you are not ready to commit. There's really nothing wrong with that; if you don't want to commit, just be straightforward.

I've been in situations where I've fully committed to a relationship and they've worked out well for the duration they were meant to. The reason they didn't go the distance was simply because I wasn't ready to take that next step or we grew apart. We both knew what the next step would have been. The relationships, in which I've straddled the fence, didn't have a chance from the onset.

When you've been single for a while, sometimes it's difficult to give up the freedom. It's difficult simply because you don't want to. You aren't ready to share your life, time, love, friends, family, bed, space, closet or anything. You don't have to check in with anyone, share your food, talk about your day, ask what's wrong or compromise any part of yourself. You don't have to share your money. You're in complete control of everything and it feels great. Sooner or later, that will begin to feel a little selfish. It's absolutely amazing when you have the opportunity to grow with the right person. You have the ability to make them a better person and vice versa.

There are certain instances, for men and women, where they may not want to get out the game. In my case, I've been single for so long that I've acquired some rather unique friendships with the opposite sex, ones that I'm not necessarily prepared to give up just for anyone. Although the friends I'm speaking of are female, I have not had sex with them. Many of the women I've talked to or began dating aren't able to process the fact that men and women can have platonic friendships. It isn't any different than a woman having a man as a best friend. Some of my best friendships are with those of the opposite sex therefore, it's going to take a very confident and sound woman to be with me and accept my friendships unless she has valid reasons not to. As long as my friend or I have done nothing to disrespect the person I'm dating, it shouldn't be a problem.

I've been single and available for almost two years. I've dated here and there but I've not been given cause to consider anything more serious. Sofia caught my attention so we began talking to get to know one another. Although she was a couple years younger, I thought she presented herself in a rather mature manner. It didn't take long before I discovered that I was mistaken.

She told me she never slept with a guy on the first night or in the first few months until she got to know them. For some reason, she provided an unsolicited statement regarding her sexual history. A caution sign went on and I made it a point to avoid sexual interaction with Sofia.

One morning, Sofia saw a picture of me on my social media page with another woman and immediately jumped to an unfounded conclusion. In fact, there were two pictures of me with the same woman because both were taken on the same day. Above both photographs, I referenced that the woman next to me was an amazing friend moving back home to the East Coast. It was evident I wasn't trying to hide the friendship, particularly since it was platonic. Most men are hesitant to post a photo with another woman if they are dating someone. Nevertheless, I received a call from Sofia exhibiting a distraught demeanor over what see stumbled upon.

She told me that we were on two different pages and she wasn't going to be disrespected. She claimed that she wanted something different than I did. I found that comical, as she never asked what I wanted. We never discussed anything remotely close to intentions or set any boundaries. Yet, her next text to me proceeded by explaining it was evident I had other things going on and she didn't have time for the unnecessary games. The old me wanted to defend myself and destroy her unsubstantiated accusations, being that I did nothing wrong. After a fleeting deliberation, I decided to concede with her allegations and simply let it go. If that's what I'd have to deal with, I was the one that didn't have time. Avoid being pulled into an argument or unhealthy discussion just because the other person is in a negative state of mind.

While there are many virtuous women who chose to sustain their virginity until the time they've designated arrives, if you're not one of them, it's not necessary to say you are. You don't owe anyone an explanation. Whatever your choices are, own them.

One of the guys I played ball with was in a sexual relationship with a woman he felt compelled to talk about. He said she was filled with drama but the sex was good. At any rate, he was planning to cut her off because he wanted to settle down. He claimed he only slept with her while his main girl was away on business. He was going to end their situation by the time his girl returned. A couple of days later, she showed up to workout with him. He called her Renée. When she saw me, she dropped her head. It was Sofia. I didn't say anything, as there wasn't any reason to.

Games such as those are unwarrantable and diminish your value and integrity as a whole. We are all guilty of playing them at some point in our life, apart from whether or not it's indirect, that doesn't make them acceptable. The way you treat people outside of your relationship will carry over to the relationship. You can't hide the real you. Anything proving to be detrimental to the healthy progression of a relationship should be omitted. If you want a healthy progression, begin with honesty. Don't pretend that you don't care, leave the lies for liars and display trust. Of course, situations will arise that will be disconcerting. Ask respectful questions, address it with a calm demeanor and communicate with factual information.

If you genuinely have a problem with your significant other having platonic friendships, discuss it properly. You may realize you never had a reason to worry. On the other hand, it's possible for you to find it more problematic based on the responses given. Talking about it before it gets to the point where fights develop is the sensible thing to do. Don't complain just because you don't like it; give him or her the reason behind it so they can follow your thought process. Assume positive intent before you bring negativity to the discussion. Countless relationships, that were once beautiful, have been ruined due to poor communication.

If you want a relationship to flourish, get out the game. It's healthy to have friendships while you're dating. Be willing to show your significant other there is nothing to hide and it is strictly nonsexual. Make it evident that these friendships are harmless. If you're single, then be single. But if you're in a relationship, your loyalty lies with that person and your friends need to respect the relationship. If you've slept with someone in one of those previous relationships, that you're still friends with, your partner should be aware of this, despite how long ago it was. At least be honest enough to give them the opportunity to either be okay with it or not.

You may play the field, but what good is sharing bits and pieces of your heart with everyone? If you want true, unconditional love, you have to give up negative or immature behavior that will keep it from working. If you are remiss to leaving the game, this is why you're single.

Chapter Sixteen

The Infamous W's

As I stated at the beginning of the book, why, is a rather broad question. If you're seeking to understand something or a specific situation, you have to be prepared to delve deep, as the surface is just the beginning. If you ask someone why he or she cheated on you or doesn't love you anymore, you're giving him or her the opportunity to be vague. Any real dialogue leading to the truth will then be avoided. If you ask when the affair started, what caused them to cheat or where in the relationship they lost interest in you, you are forcing them to be specific. Those are the leading questions that will help you understand and reach the *why* behind whatever scenario you may be seeking closure.

As with anything, there is always a reason behind ones actions and that action will undoubtedly bring a reaction. As a child, when I did something wrong, Mom would remove some of my privileges. It didn't happen often, but I remember those occasions well because Mom always asked me one question. She never asked if I knew *why* she was punishing me, as that was evident. She was punishing me because she was disappointed in my behavior. What she did ask was if I knew *what* I was in trouble for. Those two questions, although similar, created two entirely different answers.

In one of my earlier relationships, I learned the power behind asking the appropriate questions. Most would ask why someone did something or why something happened. I came to understand that the why doesn't always have an explanation or negative intent behind it. Nor does it possess the truth, as it can produce a skewed perspective.

I'll never forget the setup of one particular evening. We were lying on the beach when I noticed a large wave forcing the ocean towards us. In seconds, it would claim us. I jumped up, grabbed Alexandra's hand and pulled her to a standing position. I snatched the towels just before the waves flushed across our feet.

"Thank you. I didn't see that coming," Alexandra confessed.

"You appear to be lost in your thoughts. Is there anything you care to talk about?"

Without hesitation, she turned to face me and asked, "When did you fall out of love with me?"

I was completely caught off guard and didn't know how to respond, especially since she was calm and resolute with her inquiry. She didn't make accusations or become upset, Alexandra merely asked *when*, which made me come to terms with the fact that I actually *had* fallen out of love with her. Given she asked a succinct question, I was able to convey the time frame, which in turn gave me the ability to recognize the truth behind the why. Had she just asked me why I'd fallen out of love with her, I may have avoided the truth to keep from hurting her or facing it.

If you want specificities in your relationships or life in general, then you must ask explicit questions. Don't be afraid of the truth as it can be vindicating as well as rewarding. I believe we ask *why* to avoid the truth. The truth should be the only thing that matters in the end. Whether it hurts, helps or heals, it is *the truth*. If your mindset is averse to accepting the truth and you prefer to live a lie, well, this is why you're single.

Chapter Seventeen

Closure

As with anything in life, it's pertinent to comprehend the motivation behind every decision you make, as it will affect you. Additionally, take others into consideration whether or not your choices or actions directly or indirectly have an impact on them. How can you effectively leave a relationship if you don't grasp why you're moving? Be willing to acknowledge the reasons you need to do so as it will only help you face reality.

I was an inquisitive child because I wanted to know what made things function. I constantly disassembled items although I wasn't always able to put them back together properly. What I gained was a better and sustainable understanding of how it worked in addition to what made it stop working. Upon ending a relationship, this rationalization is comparable. You may not necessarily agree with the reason the relationship is ending, but knowing what caused the malfunction will help you refrain from duplicating those mistakes and reproducing the same or similar outcome yet again. If you know what made it work then determine where the breakdown began and what caused it to erupt. Hopefully, having proper clarification will allow you to make more appropriate decisions when choosing your next relationship. In essence, it's relatively sensible to learn from your mistakes or that of someone else. Caring about the cause is a great way to evolve into a more considerate and wiser individual.

I used to think love was worth the fight but as you grow older you'll realize it's a relationship built upon trust, faith and love that's worth fighting for. It wasn't until recently that I understood the emotional distress that not having closure can bring about, even if it's from a previous relationship.

I didn't believe it made sense for a woman to want to see me only to pursue a better understanding as to the reason I didn't want to be with them. I thought talking about it could potentially cause additional heartache or dredge up unconstructive emotions. My preference was to avoid hurting someone. When it's over, it's over, so I couldn't fathom the significance of looking and searching for additional comprehension. That conversation should take place either prior to reaching the point of no return or upon the finality of the relationship.

It was late and I was unwinding from an exhausting day. I got up from the sofa and went into the kitchen for a cup of hot tea. I've always made tea with milk, which is different from most, but it helps when I need to relax before bed. At the moment I was emotionally shutting down for the day, I received a call that a friend of mine was in the area and he wanted to talk. He told me he had a great deal on his mind and wasn't sure if he was making the right decision. He ended his relationship with a woman he cared deeply about, which caused me to venture that would be the topic. I was one to make a choice without second-guessing myself. I'd stick with my gut and Josh knew that. The times I went against it didn't work out in my favor. But Josh's ex-girlfriend seemed to be making an effort to climb back over the fence.

We sat down and I listened while he did most of the talking. It had been nearly two months since he'd spoken or communicated with his ex-girlfriend because he was done and quite frankly had already moved on. However, she wasn't finished fighting. She wanted to know definitively that there was nothing left they could do to fix them. She told him she wanted to talk because she needed closure in their relationship. That was the first time a woman had actually told him she needed closure in order to move on. I advised him to agree to her request and meet her in a public place that was comfortable for both of them. Additionally, I suggested he let her know that he had already moved on so she didn't waste her time. I told him to be honest about what caused the relationship to end and when but not to turn it into a debate or game of blame.

They met at a restaurant and had a long lunch the following day. He said she looked amazing and he hadn't seen her like that in the last year of their relationship. The first fifteen minutes were a bit awkward but when she finally opened up, they sat and talked about everything. He told her that he didn't see himself being able to get over her cheating, which was the reason it was best for them to move on. He didn't want to hate her or remain angry so he ended it. She explained that she knew she'd made a mistake but thought he'd try to get past it because she is human and subjected to human error. He explained it wasn't the mistake, but the lies behind it. When lunch ended he walked her to her car. She cried in his arms and then hugged him the way she did in the beginning of their relationship. It was their final embrace. She finally gained the closure she needed.

I told Josh there was a point when I wanted closure, too. I was seeing a girl from London and she wanted me to move there, which I wasn't willing to do. I wanted to know without a doubt that I did everything possible to make the relationship work. Once we conversed and I was certain I had, I was comfortable with moving on.

I didn't realize until I grew older how essential closure is to helping place the mind at ease. The beautiful part is that this is something we can do by ourselves. We have the proclivity to think in order to have the closure we desire, it needs to be facilitated with the other person. That's entirely inaccurate and a blessing in disguise. Often, the other person will never give you the closure you need because they think you will never be able to completely move on from them. To gain closure and come to terms with any situation regardless of the severity, simply go inward. Revisit what went wrong with complete honesty and then release it.

Closure, for all intended purposes, is exactly as it sounds. It allows you to close that chapter of your life and turn the page so you can start writing again. I didn't say it wouldn't hurt or be disheartening because if it wasn't, then the relationship was void of love to begin with.

Changing your mindset and seeking closure so you can regroup, heal and move on will allow peace and happiness to come. If you refuse to let go, this is why you're single.

Chapter Eighteen

Internet Love

I've finally come to terms with the fact that meeting someone the conventional way has become thought provoking. People don't have time or want to put in significant effort to find a quality partner only to be disappointed and realize they wasted time and money. Now that I'm older, going out is no longer a necessity or desire. While I still go out to celebrate birthdays with friends occasionally hitting the scene, my chances of finding the love of my life or even a solid candidate are slim to none. For one, that's not my motivation for stepping out and secondly, those environments simply aren't always conducive to finding a suitable partner.

The typical men and women found in bars or nightclubs aren't the ones looking for love. If they are, they may emerge a bit short. When meeting someone in that type of atmosphere, we have a tendency to assume negative intent. Judging someone by his or her attire or friends is common and we can be wrong either way. I've connected with beautiful women in some pretty upscale bars and nightclubs but I've yet to have a successful or healthy relationship stemming from one. It doesn't mean it can't happen, yet I've always been cognizant of the reasons most people go to such places, myself included. I don't expect the connection to be authentic or special. It's fun and fleeting, but that's it.

Surprisingly, I have met some beautiful, intelligent, fun and confident women online. I'm not talking about on dating sites; I'm referencing social media such as Facebook, Twitter and even Instagram. When talking to several of my friends I found that they too seek the convenience of connecting with like minds.

Meeting someone on the Internet may seem daunting and I understand the reasons. If you are going to connect with people over the Internet, there are several precautionary steps that should be taken. Be aware that whenever you meet anyone, a safe outcome isn't guaranteed.

Ladies, if you begin talking with someone that you have interest in, I'd advise doing a background check if you plan to meet up with that person. If your safety and wellbeing aren't worth a fourteen-dollar background check, then you need to reevaluate your self-worth.

Out of curiosity, I spoke with men and women that meet people via social media. I learned that the easiest and most effective method for most is talking with them using FaceTime or Skype. It limits the guesswork regarding their appearance and age while revealing if the photos they post are really them. A visual can begin to eliminate some of the doubts you have as to whether or not this person actually exists, but don't stop there.

Has a friend ever set you up on a blind date? Unless your friend knows the other person particularly well, there's not much of a difference in meeting someone online. You only know what they've told you until you authenticate it. Make sure you take the time to vet them because you're still dealing with a complete stranger. If you meet someone in a bar or nightclub and exchanged contact information at the end of the night, aren't they still a stranger? At least when you find a person that you're interested in online, you have the ability to do research, make sure that's really them and find out more. Knowing something about the other person is better than not knowing anything. If they appear to be putting on a pretentious act, press delete and they're gone. When I look at a woman's profile and pictures, it speaks volumes to the type of person they are. It's more significant than they may realize. That is one of the reason's companies use social media as a resource to investigate someone prior to offering them a position. Pictures reveal what the candidate won't. They tell you what people do when they aren't around you, the type of friends they have and how they network. You can find out if they are compassionate, violent, spiritual or potentially hosting a history of rage. Glance at their movie and music list. Read their comments as they will help you better understand how they think. Make a notation of their family members and if their pictures or communication displays respect and closeness with them. All of these things will help you have a better idea of who that person actually is. Information about someone on the Internet is not private so don't feel like your meddling. Take time to protect yourself and always meet them in a public place until you get to know more about them. The same way you're able to find information on a person, if they don't appear to have much, you should be cautious just the same.

I remember the first time I told my sister that I was going on a date with a woman I'd met online. She wasn't happy about it. I explained my schedule restraints and desire to having access to learn more about a person. She asked what safety precautions I was taking and I shared them with her. After telling my sister everything I knew about the woman and how I found out, she seemed a little more comfortable with my decision. I told her that we communicated through FaceTime for several weeks and she was a close match to what I was interested in.

I connected with other women online and it was definitely a unique experience. However, texting and talking on the phone was about as far as it had gone at that point. Bella was the first woman I decided to meet in person and she was flying in from Monterey. I decided against telling any of my friends and the only person that knew was my sister. My friends rarely influenced me, but I didn't want judgment passed until I was able to give them objective feedback from the experience.

Although we felt comfortable with one another, Bella and I decided to meet in a public location. She was originally from L.A. but relocated to Carmel due to her career. Since she was familiar with the area, I told her to choose a beach so we could grab a bite then go for a walk and watch the sunset. She loved the idea and coincidentally chose Manhattan Beach, which would have been my suggestion. I offered to pick her up from the airport and drop her at the hotel to freshen up but she decided to rent a car. Bella was planning to visit some friends along with her two brothers who lived in the area. After strategizing, we decided to meet on the pier.

I was looking out across the ocean from the pier so I could see when she arrived. I considered her to be a timely individual based on the occasions we had previously set to talk and I was right. A few minutes passed when I saw her walking towards me in a white sundress with a blue and yellow floral print. At that point, there was no turning back as we were both all in. I smiled when I saw her. She was stunning and looked even better than her pictures. The camera evidently didn't convey her true beauty leaving an even nicer surprise. As I walked towards her I began my analysis.

Bella stood about five-foot-seven, appearing much shorter in her pictures. Her dark brown hair was curly and hosted light brown highlights. She attempted to hide her curvaceous body with loose clothing. Her essence and caramel complexion was similar to that of Sanaa Lathan. I walked up, introduced myself and noticed her flashing a smile. I told her it was nice to finally meet her in person before pulling her in for a hug and kissing her on both cheeks, which had cute dimples.

It didn't take long before comfortable conversation evoked a bit of genuine laughter from both of us. I asked Bella if she wanted to grab dinner, but she wasn't ready. She slipped off her sandals, tossed them in her shoulder bag and we began our walk along the beach. Time can seem motionless when you want to escape, but two hours passed and it felt as though we had only been engaged in dialogue for less than a half hour.

Our time together was refreshing. Being that Bella had spent her last few years in Monterey, she had a great deal to share. I let her talk while I listened. The sun decided to descend peacefully into the ocean so we rested on the sand and watched the magic unfold. I told her that if she paid close attention, she would she a green flash just as the sun disappeared. When it happened, I caught a glimpse of her smile as she gazed at the horizon.

It's nice when you can feel a connection with someone you've met for the first time. Sometimes it occurs faster and more naturally than getting to know them over time. If the chemistry is there, it's unmistakable and no explanation is required.

Bella and I decided to have dinner at my place the next day. I'd been talking about my culinary skills for quite some time; according to Bella, the experience was much overdue.

Everything went well because neither of us had any expectations. The time we spent talking, prior to meeting, allowed us to get a better feel for one another. We were able to determine if our backgrounds had anything in it to discourage us from moving ahead. You never know if they're hiding something such as a spouse. If you are willing to make pragmatic choices, leaving deception out of it, you'll realize someone out there is interested in knowing the real you. They don't want a false image of what you want them to think you look like. Give an honest presentation of yourself. It doesn't make sense to begin a friendship or relationship based on deception. What you do to others may come back on you in the worse way.

Be cautious when meeting people on the Internet. There are many predators and unsavory individuals out there. Talk with them until you determine if you are a good fit for one another and meet in public places. If you're disinclined to meet people in different ways, this is why you're single.

Chapter Nineteen

The Recipe For Perfection

At a young age I learned that it's difficult to ruin a creation when it comes to cooking, aside from burning it. There isn't one particular way to season food nor is there a specific recipe that must be followed in order for it to taste perfect.

I used to be afraid to rub too much seasoning on meat or that I was being so cautious I didn't use enough. I learned that when it comes to cooking, it's an art, therefore the appreciation rest solely on the palate. I absolutely love to cook for people but when it comes down to it, I prepare a meal precisely the way I like it. It's not possible to please everyone, so I don't try. Now, if they have dietary restrictions or food allergies, that's a different story. We are all individuals that have unique tastes, preferences and dislikes. Once I was able to come to terms with that, I began to enjoy cooking even more.

When it comes to finding the right man or woman for a happy and healthy relationship, it's important to align your thought process with a similar type of thinking. Find someone that has comparable characteristics and goals because the relationship must consist of more than sex. Make sure you aren't overlooking those characteristics only to continually bump heads, which may lead to heated arguments later. Initiate deeper discussions regarding finances, children, religion, friends, family, health, expectations, sports, cooking, hobbies, and anything else that affects a relationship long-term. Short-term is when everything is fun so let's move past that phase and address reality.

When I think back on some of the relationships I let go of due to the imperfections that I wouldn't tolerate, I realize how unrealistic my expectations were. What I deem as a beautiful and perfect woman might not be the same to one of my friends. When I think of beauty, I'm analyzing the overall picture, inside and out. To some, beauty may solely rest deceptively on the skin while the interior of the person is as dark as the ocean is deep. And to others with more depth, compassion and spirituality, they will see the interior of another being above all and that's where the true beauty lies. It is ones soul, instead of the outward appearance, which determines their true beauty. That is where I find perfection.

Another pertinent thing to keep in mind is although a person may be perfect for you, the situation itself might not be. One of my close friends met a man that she fell in love with, but the obstacle was simple; he was married so neither pursued anything more. A year or so later he was divorced. Due to the intricacies surrounding their divorce, the timing wasn't appropriate. Inside and out, this woman saw him as perfect for her. The flaws that others, including myself, regarded as unacceptable were actually some of the things she loved and admired most about him. A few years passed and she held firm to what she believed and ultimately, something brought them together. Watching their bond unfold, it was inevitable that they would end up together. They are happily married and have a beautiful family as they were destined to be together. They are two people that are no less than perfect for one another. The point I'm trying to convey is that perfection is not uniform. There is no formulaic methodology to perfection, only criticism for those unaccepting of what is, as it relates to them.

Sometimes people have opposing perspectives of what they view or consider perfection. What's perfect to you may not be to someone else. This is one of the first obstacles to overcome when you are considering dating. Don't fight over what you know to be true. Your perfect isn't my perfect, and more than likely, it will never be. The recipe for perfection is nothing more than what you believe it to be. Some people don't think perfection exists while others desperately search for it. What you find perfect, others with an eye for the negative will deem flawed. There are countless things that we consider perfect but when it comes to people, we are critical of them as well as ourselves. We must learn to be more accepting of people and things as they are. If you can't leave the criticism out of it, understand he or she just isn't for you. Someone else will recognize their authentic beauty. If you don't see the incredible exquisiteness in God's creations, perhaps this is why you're single.

Chapter Twenty

Radiant Experience

It has always been my understanding that anything of value gets better with time. For instance, aging wine is something that requires significant time and patience. Many of my female friends claim they prefer to date older men because they know what they want in life, are established and exude confidence. It's funny because older men typically don't get chastised for dating younger women, yet older women dating younger men seem to be media worthy for celebrities and gossip for anyone else.

When it comes to dating an older woman, I feel the same way women do that date older men. They know what they want in a relationship and life in general. They won't tolerate any sort of nonsense because they can see through it and more likely than not, have already been through it. They have a caring and encouraging affinity. When dating an older woman, the positives most definitely outweigh the negatives. In all my years of dating, I've only dated a few women that were younger than me. Aside from the usual hiccups that come with dating in general, dating mature women has been a pleasant and intellectually stimulating experience.

While I agree that age can simply be a number and state-of-mind, it depends on the maturity and behavior of both individuals to handle the relationship. When you're beyond a ten-year range, things may start to get a bit more complicated but it doesn't mean it won't work.

Some of the other factors that should be considered are older men or women that want children, have health issues and the ability to be as physically active as you'd like. Until you determine the purpose for pursuing relationships with someone older than you, the relationship may be nothing more than a hidden little secret or timed affair. If you've had issues with your parents or lacked love from them you may be seeking an unhealthy parental type of love and if this is the case, this is why you're single.

Chapter Twenty-One

Misery Loves Company

We've all had one friend, that if they were going down, we naïvely made the choice to go right along with them. When I was younger, that didn't make much sense to me so I'd step back and evaluate situations along with the mindset of my friend at that time. I've watched many loyal women follow their friends, boyfriends and husbands into darkness without knowledge of the whole truth. I've watched women attempting to be supportive of their relationship but end up fighting a battle that was never intended for them to win. Ultimately, the aftermath to their life was financially or emotionally devastating.

Despite the adversity we encounter, we should want others to be happy. However, there are those that don't share positive streams of energy as honest sentiments. With age comes wisdom and I've developed a much sharper and simplistic perspective. Misery loves company; so don't extend the invitation to anyone. When someone is hurt, instinctively they want others to feel their pain because some people don't want to go through a stressful situation alone. It's not always intentional but if you're the closest person to them, sometimes you become a casualty of their negative state of mind.

Adversity is inevitable but the key is when it happens, seek support rather than vengeance. I typically choose to vent or discuss situations with my mother to avoid subjecting anyone else to the unconstructive dilemma that may be upon my shoulders at the moment. She is one of the few people that understands me irrespective of how I elect to convey my feelings. She knows my heart. Not everyone will identify with you or know your intent. Occasionally, the depth of your negativity or complaints can drag someone else down even if it's unintentional. If you have something that is resting heavily on your heart, take the problem to the person that understands you best. They may not have the resolution but at least they will listen because they care about you. If you are someone that's private and doesn't have anyone close enough to talk to other than the person you typically hurt with your negative communication, then talk to God. God is always listening. Make time to step aside and give God all of your anger, worries and anything else you have because God can handle it. Few have the strength to carry what is breaking you down so give it to God.

Sometimes when you take your issues to someone you love, you're more likely to hurl your problems at them because you feel entitled to the release of emotion it brings to you. You know they will take it *out of love*. But what you are doing to them is selfish and unfair. It's not healthy and you have to find another way to communicate. If it's not you, the person inflicting the misery needs to know that you don't want that type of negative communication. Yes, it's good to help the other person but when misery loves company and it becomes destructive to you, think again. You may want to suggest a visit to a therapist.

Don't allow your negativity to latch onto anyone else because it's a cowardly action. Learn to handle it appropriately. My mother has this amazing ability to extract negativity out of me. I don't have to do anything other than tell her what's going on because she listens. When I need her opinion, her communication and advice comes without judgment. What I'm saying is, it helps to have someone that *can* handle your issues. If you are in a relationship and you can't do this respectfully with your significant other, that could be a problem as trust, respect, patience and understanding are critical too.

You should learn to be cognizant and cautious of the person you confide in. As well, be vigilant of the person that openly gives you advice they haven't practiced in their own life. Are they happily married or currently going through a divorce? Are they in a healthy relationship or does their boyfriend cheat on them? Is their anger or bitterness targeting you? Are they genuinely happy for you? Repeatedly, we surround ourselves with what I like to call, subtractions. People that subtract from your life instead of adding to it will only bring harm to you. They stay around until you're physically and emotionally drained of everything you need to be happy. They take all of the positivity you have to offer and in the process, transfer their negative energy to you. Good luck with them!

Sharing achievements and joy is imperative to having a healthy relationship. Don't be so quick to spew out negativity before working to resolve the issue. Most people crave positive information as opposed to the same negative and unyielding line of conversation. Surround yourself with people that only want to see you happy and successful.

Whether it's intentional or inadvertent, people instinctively resent what they don't have or haven't accomplished. It's not to say they aren't happy for you; their happiness isn't necessarily pure and genuine because it can cause a deeper reflection of their own failures or inability to achieve what they want.

Relationships will have their struggles. You should view fighting through difficult times and creating an even stronger bond as progress. Everyone has moments where things hit a little harder. If you are constantly in turmoil, perhaps proper guidance should be considered. Don't remain the miserable person always seeking company so you can rip someone apart. If you intentionally bring others down for self-gratification, you are living in a world no one wants to enter and maybe, this is why you're single.

Chapter Twenty-Two

So You're Single

Single seems to have a negative connotation. However, it shouldn't be because you don't need to provide anyone with a reason as to *why* you are single when it is your choice.

My mother was happily single for many years. When someone would ask her why she was single her enthusiast response made me smile because to her, a relationship meant more than a status. It meant trust, love, dedication, respect, faith and all the real aspects necessary to make it work the right way. Mom said, "I won't compromise my happiness and freedom for a gamble. If you need an explanation, I'm single because I want to be." Her smile said it all!

I came to understand that being alone doesn't mean you are lonely. Nor does it denote you need another person to complete you. By the time I knew that Mom was well aware of her value, I realized it would take someone that valued and loved her the way she loved herself. The only person that could do that was a man who knew his value and loved himself. He needed to have similar attributes as Mom. That's what it would take for Mom to meet her twin flame or soul mate. She spent her time working hard, laughing from her soul, cooking with love, writing with passion and more importantly, raising my sister and I. She's always been a great inspiration to my sister and I because she taught us how to be happy. She is passionate about her career and gives my sister and I every ounce of love she has. She is a lover of life who takes in as much as she can. My sister and I learned that from her too.

If it's your preference to be single, enjoy life because it has a great deal of lessons and offers an abundance of inspiration to motivate us. Don't settle for anything less than you desire, but be the standard that you are seeking. Being happy is your choice and being single is another beautiful option. As long as you are happy, if this is why you're single, be single!